AF624719

Teaching of Geeta

OrangeBooks Publication

1st Floor, Rajhans Arcade, Mall Road, Kohka, Bhilai, Chhattisgarh 490020
Website: **www.orangebooks.in**

© Copyright, 2025, Author

All rights reserved. No part of this book may be reproduced, stored in a retrieval system, or transmitted, in any form by any means, electronic, mechanical, magnetic, optical, chemical, manual, photocopying, recording or otherwise, without the prior written consent of its writer.

First Edition, 2025

ISBN: 978-93-6554-700-9

Price: Rs. 320.00

The opinions/ contents expressed in this book are solely of the author and do not represent the opinions/ standings/ thoughts of OrangeBooks.

Printed in India

TEACHING OF GEETA

IN VIEW OF A SCIENTIST

DR. ASHOK M. BIRADAR

OrangeBooks Publication
www.orangebooks.in

Contents

Introduction

We believe that in all the living languages of the world, there is no book so full of true knowledge, and yet handy as the Bhagwat-*Geeta*. It brings to men the highest knowledge, the purest love and most luminous action. It teaches self-control, the truth, compassion and obedience to the call of duty for the sake of duty and putting up a fight against unrighteousness (अधर्म). There is no book in the whole range of the world's literature so high above all as the Bhagwat-*Geeta*, which is a treasure-house of *Dharma* (ethics) for all mankind.

Geeta is an intrinsic part of the entire *Mahabharata*, and the classic would have been a disjointed story, without pith (essence) and dignity, if Bhagwat-*Geeta* was not in it – and the *Geeta* would have been a mere philosopher's riddle-poem without the *Mahabhharata* background. The story and the poem together are in an organic whole; each devoid of the other would be ineffectual and empty. If we try to properly digest the implications of the *Geeta's* advice, it becomes amply clear how actions performed without egocentric desires purge the mind of its deep-seats and prepare for greater fights into the infinite beyond.

Who can take advantage of Geeta?

One side of life is dreams of worldly (संसार) affairs, up and down in life, happy and unhappy, and satisfaction of sense-organs and the other side of life is to seek the realities in this life (संसार). The person controlling the sense-organs can only try to seek the solution in life between these two aspects and will get the solutions from the Bhagwat-*Geeta*. As such, *Geeta* is not a costly book, and anybody can purchase and read it. However, reading any philosophical book is of no use. It has to be read and tried to apply in real life, then only it will have an advantage. The *Geeta* book cannot be read by *Tamsic*-nature (असुरी-प्रकर्ति) people because of their egotism and no ethics in life. The people who have *Sattvic-Guna* (pureness in thoughts) can take the tremendous advantage from the *Geeta*'s teachings in life.

Bhagwat-*Geeta* is for those who think through their consciousness (मंथन or चिंतन) and whose intelligence (बुद्धि) is pure. Many times the consciousness is covered by our excessive attachment (मोह), egoness (अहंकार) and desire (कामना), and we don't make the right decision. Similar is the case with Arjuna, his attachment overtook his consciousness and he decided not to fight in the war. But his teacher (Lord Krishna) regained his consciousness by giving the advice mentioned in the *Geeta*, and then he (Arjuna) regained his consciousness and decided to fight in the war. If you don't think through consciousness, then it does not mean that you cannot read the *Geeta.* One can read it particularly for

Rajassic (passionate) quality people, slowly and slowly, they start thinking through consciousness and raise themselves to the *Sattvic*-quality *Gunas* and spend a peaceful life. Many people make it a routine to read the *Geeta* daily without understanding its meaning which is of no use. When they go to the market place, their egoness, desire, and attachment overcome their consciousness. Therefore, reading the advice of *Geeta* and following them in day- to - day life is important and useful. This advice cannot be followed in one day, but slowly and slowly with self-introspection, one can spend a happy and contented life in light of Bhagwat-*Geeta.*

Vital questions in life

In this worldly affair (संसार), we face many difficulties, and we want to have answers for them. These are our mental issues. Men are not satisfied only with food to eat, although food, shelter to live is essential for survival, like any other living being. If these basic things for survival are not satisfied, his mind (मन) cannot think of mental issues. Once they (essential things) are satisfied, human beings think about mental issues, regarding life. And therefore, many religions are born in this world. One religion or one sect cannot satisfy the needs of all human beings related to mental issues. It is not wrong to have a different religion because of the fact that in different regions or environments, the mental issues vary. However, the common questions are: What is the purpose of life? What is the secret of life? Is it taking the birth and having children, and then becoming old and finally dying, is it the purpose of life? These questions arise in everybody's life, which is not wrong; otherwise, the progress of men hinders. At a young age, these questions, regarding the purpose of life, don't disturb us as we are busy in our worldly affairs (संसार), making wealth for the future and enjoyment in materialistic things. However, in old age, particularly worldly affairs decrease, and then the question of life purpose starts cropping up in our mind.

What is the purpose of life? Men try to find out answers to such questions, and until he gets its answer, he cannot go ahead. It is not necessary that our questions can be philosophical, but a small issue in life can help us go ahead in life. We may try to ignore such issues by keeping ourselves in work for the time being, but such questions arise in our mind and disturb us. Such a question is not only in India but all over the world. In the developed Western world, where science has improved life quality substantially, there also such questions arise, regarding the purpose of life. A Nobel-winner, Eleksis Kerl, writes in his book entitled "Men the unknown" that he raises such questions regarding the purpose of life. He says that Man has two personalities, one is known and another is unknown. The known personality is his height, colour, face means outer personality. But the other personality is completely unknown, like his thinking process, his behaviour and many other things. Further, he writes in his book that knowing the unknown personality in humans or in himself, is life. He also writes that we do not know even one per cent of our own inner personality. Does it mean that we cannot know our own inner personality? How can we do it?

In India a lot of research work was done for the above questions in the good olden days by the *Rushis* (Saints). We can know the materialistic world by the sense-organs like our body parts, through the eyes, sound through the ears, smell by the nose and sensation through the skin, but we cannot know through these sense-organs, regarding the mind or inner thinking process of the human. However, we can get the knowledge of the mind's thinking process by the mind alone. How do we do it? The first thing is to try to understand the mind, and judge it carefully. The ancient Saints (ऋशी) in India tried to understand the mind. When the mind is in sleep, we do not feel happiness or sorrow and as soon as it (mind) is awake, we feel the feelings of thought. These saints in the old days researched and came to conclusions that yes, we can understand the mind, and that process is called "*Gyan*-Yoga."

In the Bhagwat-*Geeta* the process of knowing the mind through Yoga is given very beautifully. What is Yoga? Yoga is nothing but controlling the sense-organs through the mind only; otherwise, our mind always runs through our sense-organs. It (mind) runs when we are awake or even in the sleep of dreaming about something, and it never goes into a zero state. But in deep sleep, the mind goes into a zero state, but here the mind is also sleeping. Therefore, we cannot know the mind's knowledge. The man's mind continuously runs through the sense-organs which can be controlled and directed in one direction by knowledge only, and that knowledge is called "*Gyan*-Yoga," given in the *Geeta.*

Why are Karmas (actions) necessary?

Geeta has given a technique for doing the *Karmas* to the human race, where one can do the *Karmas* and attain the highest on the spiritual plane, which is applicable for all types of work. For human survival and for wealth creation, we have to struggle day and night and face many difficulties, resulting in ups and downs in life. A labourer does the hard physical work, a businessman does the business, an intellectual does the mental work and a woman does the work at home. All types of this work are nothing but the *Karmas* (action) only. Lord Krishna has shown that by doing such work or *karmas* how one can spend a happy and peaceful life by sacrificing the *Karmas* to the Almighty (*Ishwar*), which He (Lord) called as *yajna* (यज्ञ) in the *Geeta* and used in the Vedas also. *Yajna* (यज्ञ) is defined in the Veda as sacrificing food, wood or even animals in the fire to please the Gods for attaining heaven. This practice still exists in the Indian sub-continent. This type of *Yajna* was very expensive; therefore, it was not possible for poor and common people. Lord Krishna opposed this idea. But he used the *Yajna* term in a new way and defined the *Yajna* (यज्ञ) for sacrificing the *Karmas* to the Almighty (God), where poor and common people also can take advantage of it. For *Nishkam-Karmas* He used the word *Yajna* (यज्ञ). All the *Karmas* have a binding effect on a man due to the fruits of action. If the same *Karma* done with *Yajna* (यज्ञ) in the mind becomes unbinding.

What does it mean by doing *Karmas* as *Yajna* (यज्ञ)? Do all *Karmas* become *Yajna*? If one does the bad *Karmas* (दुश-कर्मा) and dedicates to the Almighty (ईश्वर), do those *Karmas* also become *Yajna*? No, Lord Krishna defines three forms of *Karmas* i.e. *Karmas* (कर्म), *Vikarma* (विकर्म) and *Akarma* (अकर्म). *Vikarma* is prohibited, which is not good for oneself or society or for the nation. The *Akarma* means not doing any *Karma* due to laziness and inertness, which is generally observed in *Tamssic*-nature people. Therefore in the Bhagwat-*Geeta,* the *Karmas* done with ethics (नैतिक) and as a duty for himself and for the society can become a *Yajna* (यज्ञ). A man should do introspection for his past mistakes and raise himself. Man can become his friend and his enemy. However, most of the time, people blame others and the circumstances for their failure, which is not the truth. Therefore, Lord Krishna says that do such *Karmas* where you lift yourself (friend) and avoid such *Karmas* where you sink yourself (शत्रु). Secondly, He also advises that try to do social work, such as natural disasters or calamities or social gatherings, and such *Karma* does not have any binding effect on a person.

Everybody wants peace in worldly affairs (संसार). But this worldly affair towards family and towards society is completely a mess (झमेला). It is very difficult to have peace of mind. However, Lord Krishna says that by living in the same worldly affairs (संसार), you can have peace of mind, but you have to change your way

(द्रष्टिकोण) of doing *Karmas*. You do your *Karmas* or duties as a sacrifice (यज्ञ) and your desire, attachment, and ego as minimally as possible then in the same worldly affairs (संसार) you can have peace of mind and spend a satisfied and contented life.

Two viewpoints of doing *Karmas*: Let us take the example of two persons of thinking processes of doing *Karmas*. One believes in God (ईश्वर). And another person does not believe in God, and thinks that because of his hard work and his intelligence, he does his *Karmas* and then I should get my work's benifit. Therefore, he thinks I myself is responsible for the fruits of my actions and God (ईश्वर) does not come into the picture. The person who believes in God thinks that I should do my K*armas* and the rest he leaves to God. Now, let us say both of them got success in their *Karmas* (work). The person who does not believe in God thinks that because of his hard work and strength and intelligence, I was successful, and this way his egotism increases. The second person who believes in God thinks that it is God's blessing and he dedicates his success to God. From outside, we don't see any difference between these two people's personalities, but from inside, the person who does not believe in God, his egotism is increased. And the person who believes in God becomes softer and polite and thinks it is God's grace. Now if both persons become failures in their work *(Karmas)*. The person who does not believe in God blames his failure on his friends or on the circumstances and becomes dejected in life. There are cases in society, some people cannot digest the failure and take the extreme step of committing suicide. The person who believes in God thinks his failure is God's wish, and again he thinks God might have some plans for my failure and works hard in the work (*Karmas*) and goes ahead in life. These are two views of doing *Karmas* (actions) in the world, and there is no third view of doing *Karmas*.

What is Swadharma (स्वधर्म)?

In the Indian context "*Dharma*" is used in many ways; therefore, it creates some confusion. It is used for religious purposes like Hindu, Christian or Islamic *Dharma*, or it is being used even for sub-casts like Khetriya, Vaishas or Brahman *Dharma*. In Bhagwat-*Geeta* (ch.4-13), the *Swadharma* (स्वधर्म) was defined on the basis of *Gunas* and *Karmas* and not on the basis of birth. Even for a profession for a longer duration, and if he becomes an expert in that field, like teaching (teachers) or medical work (doctors), then it (work) becomes his *Dharma;* in other words, that particular profession is in his *Gunas* and called his *Dharmas*. *Dharma* is also defined as duty, for example, parents have the duty towards their children to give a good education and take the proper care which means it is the parents' *Dharma* towards their children.

The *Swadharma* is very important, which is applicable in today's era also. There are mainly two layers of *Swadharma*, one is from inside and another is from outside. The inside layer defines your mental get-up or aptitude, which also comes from one's past birth. The outside layer depends upon your family background (or cast). If a boy wants to become a soldier and his family background is also in defence, then it is easy for him to go into defence, or we call it *Swadharma*. A boy has an interest in business, and his background is from a doctor's family, then it is not his *Swadharma* for him. If we think of Arjuna, Bhima or Duryodhana, their family background was of a royal family, and their aptitude (interest) was also in fighting, so it is their *Swadharma* However, Yudhishtra's aptitude was in knowledge (spirituality), but he was forced into war; therefore, it was not his *Swadharma* in the *Mahabharta.*

You may feel another's *Dharma* (work) attractive and start doing work (परधर्म), which is called abandoning *Swadharma* (स्वधर्म-त्याग), generally, you end up with failure. For example, an engineer works in the IT profession for a long time, which becomes his *Swadharma*, and he feels acting profession is better profession (परधर्म), so he quits his job and starts working in the film industry, but generally he ends with failure. You may think that a child has an interest in some work, but when he grows, his interest changes and he works in some other field. Such a change in *Karmas* is not called abandoning *Swadharma* but mental progress (मानसिक-विकास). No *Dharma* in this whole world is perfect. All *Dharma* have advantages and disadvantages. Then the question arises, how do we keep ourselves happy and contented in our *Dharma*? Lord Krishna says in the *Geeta* that you stick to your own *Dharma* and do your duties (कर्मा) and leave the fruits of action to the Almighty, but don't reverse the action, which means don't leave the doer ship (कर्तापन) to the Lord and fruits in your hand. Then another question comes if you do the bad *Karmas* (विकर्म) and leave the fruits of action to God. Lord Krishna says such *Karmas* (विकर्म and अकर्म) should not be done. These are the characteristics of *Tamssic*-people (असुरी-प्रकर्ति).

Peace in mind is Eternal

Bhagwat-*Geeta's* advice is that by changing the external things, like changing the place or changing the material things, we cannot get mental peace. The changes have to be done or made from inside, which means in our mind (मन). Our point of view (द्रष्टिकोण) has to be changed towards materialistic things then only we can have mental peace. Even if we go to the quiet place like the jungle or a remote place or a hill station, we cannot get mental peace because our disturbed mind is always with us. It is not wrong to go to a quiet place like the hills or jungles. But can we spend a peaceful time there for a long time? Few days we can spend time sightseeing and doing other things. One can spend time only in meditation or deep thinking in a quiet place. But the question arise, do we have the right (अधिकारी) for meditation?

The question arises, then, how do we get mental peace (शांति)? For this, we have to identify the internal enemy first and then try to rectify it. Lord Krishna says that our eternal enemies are excessive desire (कामना), anger (क्रोध), ego (अहंकार), attachments (मोह), etc. If we can control these enemies in our own mind and intelligence, then we can have the right to peace. These enemies cannot be removed in a day or two but need continuous practice in our own lives. Whenever such an enemy appears in our daily life, try to do self-introspection and try to avoid it in future. Our main problem is that we think of ourselves as intellectual (पंडित), but we never follow in our actual day-to-day behaviour, which is the main reason for our unhappiness. Unless and until we catch up to our own weaknesses as explained above, we cannot expect any peace in our mind and any quiet place or any jungle, or any religious place will not help us with our unhappiness in life. Ramkrishna Parmhans says that in the present time (कलि-युग), the main reason for unhappiness is that our mind (मन) and our speech (मुख) are totally different (द्वन्द्व), in worldly affairs, resulting in unhappiness. Again, he says that a man can be awakened if he is sleeping, but if a man is pretending to sleep, it is very difficult to awaken him.

Justice (धर्म) also should be aggressive (क्रूर)

As all of us know, unethical (अधार्मिक) people are aggressive and violent. They keep the people under their control by force. Unethical (अधर्म) things work only with fear and force. But the ethical people (धार्मिक) by nature are soft and not aggressive. Their organisation is cool. Ethical people are goody-goody in nature and well in behaviour and helpful to others. However, when they see unethical people doing wrong things to others, they don't indulge but go away from the sense. Lord Krishna in Bhagwat-*Geeta* says that for protecting ethics (धर्म), the ethical people also should be aggressive to stop the unethical things. Therefore, Lord Krishna says to Arjuna to leave aside attachment (मोह) and fight for the ethical (*Dharma*) things. If Arjuna does not fight the war, the *Mahabharta* war also might not have taken place, and Duryodhana would have set up an unethical kingdom. And people would say that truth does not have victory or justice does not get victory, and only injustice wins. Therefore, Krishna tells Arjuna to fight for the ethical (*Dharma*) things, although many soldiers will be killed in the war, but establishing an ethical kingdom is more important than lives. This is also applicable in our daily life.

Author's experience in light of Bhagwat-Geeta

The author is an honorary scientist (retired) at the National Physical Laboratory, New Delhi. He is from the remote place of Bhalki in Karnataka state, India. He is from a farmer's family of the lower middle class. His education was from Bhalki (Karnataka), Aurangabad, now Sambhaji Nagar (Maharashtra) and V.V.Nagar (Gujarat). After finishing his Ph.D. degree, he joined as a scientist at the National Physical Laboratory, New Delhi and worked in research activities in physics for more than 35 years. He was not an intelligent student, but because of his hard work, he always stood among the first five students in the class. He was not a religious person from the beginning. However, he was an ethical living throughout his life.

After his retirement, there were no family responsibilities and no official work, he got a lot of time to spend on his own interests. His first interest was in scientific invention, and his second interest was in spirituality. Therefore, half of the day he used to spend on spirituality and half the time on scientific inventions. The first thing that came to his mind, regarding spirituality, was the Bhagwat-*Geeta*. He never read the *Geeta* until he was in a job, but heard from different people, regarding Bhagwat-*Geeta's* advice. His main problem was, he did not know the *Sanskrit* language. Whatever knowledge he acquired was from English versions of the Bhagwat-*Geeta.* He became a member of the Delhi Public Library and used to get the related book on the *Geeta*. He read the first book entitled "Bhagwat-*Geeta* for scientists", written by Prof. M.S. Manhas of the USA. Then he read four, five books on the *Geeta.* After digesting some of the teachings from the *Geeta,* and tried to apply them in his own life. He got very good results, which is a contented and happy life. As written in the *Geeta* the First thing is *Karma* (action) without expecting fruits of action (*Nishkam-Karmas*), secondly, the main enemies of our embodiment (mind) are excessive desires, ego, attachment, anger and how to control them.

Another important aspect in his life based on Bhagwat-*Geeta*'s teaching is that he started believing in the re-birth theory, which he never believed as a scientist.

When he was young age of 10, 11 years old, his father decided to make him a *Maharaja* (priest) in a temple, as the temple had a lot of agricultural property. He also accepted his father's advice because his family's financial condition was very bad and he thought the financial condition would be better. That means it was a perfect condition to adopt the *Bhakti*-path or *Sannyasi* for him, but he never liked this path and wanted to have knowledge - based studies. He persuaded his family and went away from the town to do further studies and earned a doctorate in physical sciences. However, whenever he went to his home town he always used to tell his father or brother to do something for the common people from the temple's income, but they never listened to him and used to satisfy their selfish means only.

The question arises why he (author) has written all his personal things? Because he never believed in the re-birth theory. However, knowingly or unknowingly, he was doing ethical *Karmas* but *Sakam-Karmas* (सकाम) only, with family-related motives. Then, after his retirement, what prompted him to do the *Nishkam-Karmas* (निष्काम-कर्मा or without fruits)? It is the Bhagwat-*Geeta's* teachings. That means he has seeds inside his soul for *Nishkam-Karmas* and the knowledge, but it was in dormant condition, which must have come from the past life only. That's how, with his own experience, he believes in the re-birth theory and whenever any verse appears particularly in chapter 2 of Bhagwat-*Geeta*, he tries to explain the re-birth theory and aspects of life scientifically.

Conclusion

Bhagwat-*Geeta* gives us how to spend a happy and contented life in worldly affairs (संसार). *Geeta* mainly described the *Karmas* (action) and *Gyan* (Knowledge) Yoga, particularly in chapter-2 in abstract form and then explained in detail in subsequent chapters. However, *Bhakti*-Yoga and *Sannyasa-Marg* are also given in some of the chapters of the *Geeta*. The description is not only from the spiritualistic (अध्यात्मिक) point of view, but the materialistic view is also given in detail. Life is nothing but a combination of materialistic and spiritual processes. If these two components are in good condition, then we can spend a peaceful life by controlling our eternal enemies, which is beautifully explained in the *Geeta.* The eternal enemies are ego (अहंकार), excessive desire (कामना), attachments (मोह), anger (क्रोध), etc. Not only the enemies are described, but remedies to control them are also explained in Bhagwat-*Geeta*. If you can control these two components of materialistic things, which are done by *Karma*-Yoga and the spiritualistic process effectively, then one can become *Gyan*-Yogi (स्थितप्रज्ञ).

In this book, the *Sanskrit* Shlokas (verses) of Bhagwat-*Geeta* were directly translated into English and Hindi languages for the well-educated and common people. In the text, difficult words in English or no equivalent English words are mentioned in Hindi and Sanskrit in Italic form.

Chapter - 1

Arjuna's Grief – Introduction

No other race in the world had ever harnessed so successfully the scintillating possibilities of ethics *(Dharma)* in literature for the purpose of philosophical exposition. The *Upanishads* were recorded in the form of conversation between the teacher and student, in the quiet atmosphere of the silent and peaceful Himalayan valleys. In the Bhagwat-*Geeta*, however, the highest and the best philosophy has been reiterated, in a more elaborate and detailed dramatic layout amidst the din and roar of a total war. The Lord Krishna gives his message of manly-action to Arjuna amidst the breathing, palpitating environment of the clash and carnage of the battlefield.

The *Kauravas, a* hundred in number, represent the innumerable ungodly forces of negative tendencies within man's bosom, and the *Pandavas*, no doubt, represent the divine impulses in them. A constant *Mahabharata* war is being waged within every one of us at all our crucial moments of action; and in all cases, the negative forces in each one of us are larger in number and usually mightier in their effectiveness, while the inner divine army is ever smaller in number and apparently, comparatively weaker in efficiency. Therefore, every single individual, at the moment of his inward checking up, must necessarily feel the desperation of Arjuna.

The story of the *Mahabharata* sounds an optimistic note of hope to man that, even though the diviner impulses are seemingly less in number, if the same are organised fully and brought under the guidance, of the supreme Lord, Krishna, the self (*Atama*); then, under His guidance, they can easily be ushered into a true and permanent victory over the outnumbering forces of lust and greed.

In *Sanskrit* works, it is a recognised tradition that the opening stanza should generally indicate the whole theme of the text. The bulk of the book then discusses at length the different views and gives all possible arguments, until in its concluding portion, the last stanza generally summarises the conclusions of the *Shastra* on the theme indicated in the opening section of the book. In this way, when we consider the *Geeta*, we find that the Divine song starts with the word *'DHARMA'* and concludes with the term "MINE' *(Mama)*; and therefore, the contents of the *Geeta* – we may conclude – are nothing but 'MY *DHARMA' (Mama Dharma).*

Dharma means, therefore, not merely righteousness or goodness, but it indicates the essential nature of anything, without which it cannot retain its independent existence. For example, a cold, dark sun is impossible, as heat and light are the *Dharma* of the sun. Similarly, if we are to live as truly dynamic men in the world, we can only do so by being faithful to our true nature, and the *Geeta* explains to me 'My *Dharma'*.

Dhritrashtra said:

1. What did the sons of Pandu and also my people do when, desirous to fight, they assembled together on the holy plain of Kurukshetra, O Sanjaya?

"ध्रतराष्ट्र बोले – हे संजय ! कुरुक्षेत्र के धर्मक्षेत्र में युद्ध करने की इच्छा से इकठा होकर मेरे लोगों और पांडवो ने क्या किया ? "

In the entire *Geeta,* this is the only verse that the blind old king Dhritrashtra gives out. All the rest of the verses are Sanjaya's report on what happened on the Kurukshetra battlefield, just before the war. He asks Sanjaya to explain to him what is happening on the battlefield of Kurukshetra. Vyasa had given Sanjaya the powers to see and listen to the happenings in far-off Kurukshetra even while he was sitting beside Dhritarashtra in the palace at Hastinapur.

Battlefield description

Sanjaya Said:

2. Having seen the army of the *Pandavas* drawn up in battle array, King Duryodhana then approached his teacher (Drona) and spoke these words.

"संजय बोला – किन्तु तब पांड्वो की सेना को व्यूहद्ध देखकर राजा दुर्योधन आचार्य द्रोंण के पास जा ऐसे वचन बोला –"

From this stanza onwards, we have the report of Sanjaya upon what he saw and heard on the warfront at Kurukshetra. As a child would run to its parents in fright, Durodhana, unsettled in his mind, runs to his teacher, Dronacharya. When our motives are impure and our cause unjust, however well equipped we may be, our minds necessarily feel restless and agitated. This is the mental condition of all tyrants and lusty dictators.

3. Behold, O Teacher! This mighty army of the sons of Pandu, arrayed by the son of Drupada, thy wise disciple.

"हे गुरुदेव! आप अपने बुद्धिमान शिष्य द्रुपद-पुत्र धृष्टयुम्न के द्वारा व्यूह में रची गयी पांडवो की विराट सेना को देखिये I"

It is indeed stupid of Duryodhana to point out to Drona the army formation of the *Pandavas*. Later on, we shall find Duryodhana talking too much, and that is a perfect symptom indicating the inward fears of the great king over the final outcome of the unjust war.

4. Here are the heroes, mighty archers, equal in battle to Bhima and Arjuna, Yuyudhana, Virata and Drupada, each commanding eleven thousand archers.

5. Dhrishtaketa, Chekitana, and the valiant king of Kashi, Purujit and Kuntibhoja and Saibya, the best of men.

6. The strong Yudhamanya and the brave Uttamaujas, the son of Subhadra and sons of Draupadi, all of them, were divisional commanders.

> "इस सेना में युद्ध करने में भीम और अर्जुन के समान बड़े-बड़े धनुर्धारी योधा है, युयुधान (सात्यकि), विराट और महारथी द्रुपद जैसे शूरवीर है, (फिर) ध्रष्टकेतु, चेकितान तथा बलवान पुरुजित, कुन्तिभोज और नरश्रेष्ट शेल्य, पराक्रमी युधमन्यु, बलवान उतमोजा, सुभद्रा-पुत्र अभिमन्यु, और द्रोपदी के पांचो पुत्र ये सब के सब महारथी है I"

In these three stanzas, we have a list of names of all those who were noted personalities in the *Pandava* army. Duryodhana is reviewing his enemies standing in formation.

7. Know also, O best of among the twice-born, the names of those who are the most distinguished amongst ourselves, the leaders of my army; these I name to thee for the information.

"हे द्विजश्रेष्ठ I हमारे पक्ष के भी जी प्रधान है, उन्हें आप समझ लीजिए। आपकी जानकारी के लिए में उनके नाम बतलाता हु, जो कि मेरी सेना के नेता है I"

8. Yourself and Bhishma, Karna and Kripacharyya. The victorious in war, Aswathama, Vikarna, and also the son of Somadatta.

"आप, पितामह भीष्म, कर्ण और रणविजयी कृपाचार्य तथा वैसे ही अश्वथामा, विकर्ण और सोमदत्त का पुत्र भूरिश्रवा I"

9. And many other heroes also who are determined to give up their lives for my sake, armed with various weapons and missiles, all well-skilled in battle.

"इनके सिवा अन्य भी बहुत से शूरवीर है, जिन्होंने मेरे लिए, अपने प्राणों का त्याग दिया है I ये सभी नाना प्रकार के शस्त्रोयो को धारण करनेवाली तथा युधविधा में निपुण है I"

Addressing his master as 'the best among the twice-born, Duryodhana now repeats the names of the distinguished heroes in his own army. The incorrigible vanity of the dictatorial honour that such a vast array of heroes had come ready to lay down their lives for 'MY SAKE'. To all careful students of *Mahabharata,* it cannot be very difficult to estimate how many of these great veterans would have thrown in their lot with Duryodhana, had it not been for the fact that Bhishma, the grandsire, was fighting in the ranks of the *Kauravas.*

10. This army of ours, defended by Bhishma, is sufficient, whereas that army of theirs, defended by Bhima, is sufficient. Or, this army of ours, protected by Bhishma, is unlimited, whereas that army of theirs, protected by Bhima, is limited.

"ऐसी वह पितामह भीष्म द्वारा रक्षित हमारी सेना अपर्याप्त है, परन्तु भीम द्वारा रक्षित इन पाण्ड्वों कि यह सेना पर्याप्त है I"

11. Therefore, do you all, stationed in your respective positions in the several divisions of the army, protect Bhishma alone.

"(तो अब) आप लोग सब, सभी मोरचों पर अपनी-अपनी जगह डटे हुए, केवल पितामह भीष्म की ही रक्षा करे I"

In the art of warfare, each army had, no doubt, a commander-in-chief, but it also had a powerful man of valour. Courage and intelligence, who functions as the 'defender'. In the *Kaurava* forces, Bhishma officiated as the 'defender', and in the *Pandava* forces, Bhima held the office. Therefore, Duryodhana is instructing his various commanders working in different wings to work out the single policy of protecting Bhishma.

12 His glorious grandsire (Bhishma), the oldest of the *Kauravas,* in order to cheer Duryodhana, now sounded aloud a lion's roar and blew his conch.

‘(त्ब) कुरुवंशियों में व्रद्ध प्रतापी पितामह भीष्म ने उस दुर्योधन के हृर्दय में हर्ष उत्पन्न करते हुए उच्च स्वर में सिह के समान गरजकर शंख बजाया I”

13. Then (following Bhishma), conches and kettledrums, tabors, drums and cow-horns blared forth quite suddenly, and the sound was tremendous.

“तत्र शंक, नगारे, ढोल, म्रदंग और रणसिंगा आदि बाजे-अचानक ही एक साथ बज ऊठे I वह आवाज भयंकर हुई I”

Bhishma was not standing, not too far away, observing the pitiable confusion of the tyrant. The revered grandsire noticed, intelligently, in Duronacharya's silence, the outraged temper of a man of knowledge and action. Understanding this psychology of officers under his command, the great Marshall, Bhishma, took up his war-bugle (conch) and blew it, sending forth roaring waves of confidence into the hearts of the people manning the array.

All the commanders were, no doubt, in high tension, and as soon as they heard the marshal's bugle, individually, each one of them took his instrument and sounded the battle-cry. Thus, conches and kettledrums, tabors and trumpets, bugles and cow-horns, all burst forth into a challenging war-call, which Sanjaya, half-heartedly, describes as tremendous.

14. Then, also Madhava and the son of Pandu, seated in their magnificent chariot, yoked with white horses, blew their divine conches.

"तब सफेद घोड़ों से युक्त बड़े भारी रथ में बैठे हुए श्रीकृष्ण और अर्जुन ने भी अपने अलोकिक शंख बजाये I"

15. Hrishikesha blew the *Panchajanya,* and Dhananjaya (Arjuna) blew the *Devadatta* and *Vrikodara* (Bhima), the doer of terrible deeds, blew the great conch, named *Paundra*.

"श्रीकृष्ण ने पांचजन्य नामक और अर्जुन ने देवदत्तं नामक शंक बजाया I भयानक कर्म करनेवाले वाघ जैसे उदरवाले भीम ने पौंड्र नामक अपना महान शंख बजाया I"

Krishna and Arjuna answered the battlecry. Here, the description-sitting in a magnificent chariot, harnessed with white horses, Madhava and Arjuna blew their conches- clearly echoes the hope lurking in the mind of Sanjaya that due to the apparent contrast in two descriptions, perhaps, even at this moment, Dhritarashtra may be persuaded to withdraw his sons from the war front. In his (Sanjaya) description of the *Pandava* array, he is very particular in mentioning even the name of each warrior's special conch. *Panchajana* was blown by Krishna (Hrishikesha).

16. King Yudhisthira, the son of Kunti, blew the *Anantavijaya;* Nakula and Sahedeva blew the *Sughosha* and the *Manipushpaka.*

> “कुन्तीपुत्र राजा युधिष्ठिर ने अनन्तविजय, नकुल ने सुघोष और सहदेव ने मणिपूश्पक नाम का शंक बजाया I”

17. The king of Kashi, an excellent archer, Shikhandi, the mighty commander of eleven thousand archers, Dhristadyumna, Virat and Satyaki, the unconquered.

> “काशी के महाराजा, शिखंडी, ध्रष्टधुम्नो, विराट और सात्यकि ने भी अपने-अपने शंख बजाए I”

18. Drupada and the sons of Draupadi, O Lord of the earth, and the son of Subhadra, the mighty armed, blew their respective conches.

"द्रुपद और द्रोपदी के पांचो पुत्र तथा महाबाहु सुभद्रापुत्र अभिमन्यु इस सब ने भी सब और से अलग-अलग शंख बजाये I"

In the above stanzas, we have the enumeration of the great *Maharathis,* battalion commander, who, with enthusiasm, loudly blew their conches, again and again, in an ascending cadence. The arrow that ultimately felled Bhishma in the *Mahabharata* war came from Shikhandi. The Charioteer of Krishna, who was also a battalion commander in the *Pandava* army, was called Satyaki.

The report is being addressed to Dhritarashtra, and it is indicated by Sanjaya's words, "Oh Lord of the earth".

19. That tumultuous and frightening uproar which shook the earth and the sky, distressed the hearts of the sons of Dhritarashtra.

"वह घोर आवाज धरती और आकाश को दहलाते हुए ध्रतराष्ट्र के पुत्रो के ह्र्यों को विदीर्ण करने लगी I"

20. Seeing the sons of Dhritarashtra properly arrayed, and when the missiles were just ready to be dropped, the *Pandava* (Arjuna), whose flag depicts *Maruti* (monkey), picked up his bow.

"तब हे राजन I ध्रतराष्ट्र-पक्ष के सैनिकों को खड़े देखकर ठीक शस्त्र छूटने के समय कपिध्वज अर्जुन ने अपना धनुष उठाकर श्रीकृष्ण से यों वचन कहेंI"

In these verses, we have a description of the arrival of the hero of the *Mahabharata* war, Arjuna, on the battlefield. The exact time and nature of his entry are noted here. The shooting had not yet started, but it was imminent. It was the most tense moment that Arjuna, whose ensign was that of *Hanuman,* said the following words to Lord Krishna.

Arjuna said:

21. Amid the two armies, place my chariot, O Achyuta.

22. That I may behold those who stand here desirous of fighting, and, on the eve of this battle, let me know with whom I must fight.

"अर्जुन बोला – हे अच्युत I क्रपया मेरा रथ दोनों सेनाओं के बीच में ले जाकर खड़ा कर दे, जिससे में युद्ध की कामना से खड़े इन लोगों को देख लू और जान लू कि इस युद्ध में मुझे किनके साथ लड़ना है I"

23. For I desire to observe those who are assembled here for the fight, wishing to place in battle, the evil-minded sons of Dhritarashtra.

"दुर्बुद्धि दुर्योधन का युद्ध में कल्याण चाहने वाले ये जो राजा लोग यहा इखट्टे हुए है, उन युद्ध करने वालों को में देखना चाहता हु I"

Here, we hear Arjuna's soldier-like command to the charioteer to drive and place the vehicle between the two armies so that he might see and recognise the various heroes whom he has to meet and fight in the Great war. In expressing thus a wish to review the enemy lines, the great hero is showing his daring and chivalry, his great courage and firm determination, his adventurous readiness and energy. Up to this point in the story, Arjuna, the invisible hero of the *Mahabharata,* was in his true element, unaffected by any mental hysteria.

Krishna said:

24. Thus, addressed by Gudakesha, O *Bharata*, Hrishikesha, having stationed the best of chariots between the two armies;

25. In front of Bhishma and Drona, and all the rulers of the earth, he said, "O *Partha*, behold these *Kurus* gather together."

"संजय बोले – हे गुडाकेशेनं I अर्जुन द्वारा इस प्रकार कहे जानेपर श्रीकृष्ण ने उस सर्वश्रेष्ट रथ को दोनों सेनाओं के बिच में, भीष्म, द्रोंण एवं सभी राजाओं के सामने ले जाकर खड़ा कर दिया और अर्जुन से कहा – पार्थ इन इकठ्ठे हुए कौरवों को देख I"

At a point facing Bhishma, Drona and all the rulers of the earth, the Divine charioteer pulled up the reins and brought the royal chariot to a halt. As a dutiful driver, Krishna says to Arjuna, “Behold, O’ *Partha!* All the *Kauravas* gathered together.” These are the only words that Krishna has spoken in the entire chapter.

26. Then *Partha* was stationed there in both armies, fathers, grandfathers, teachers, maternal uncles, brothers, sons, grandsons and friends too.

“तब प्रथापुत्र अर्जुन ने उन दोनों ही सेना में स्थित हुए, अपने ताऊओ-चाचाओ, पितामहो, आचार्यो, मामाओ, भाइयों, पुत्रों, पोत्रो तथा मित्रों, ससुरों और सुम्ह्दो को भी देखा I”

27. He saw fathers-in-law and friends also in both the armies. Then the son of Kunti, seeing all these kinsmen thus standing arrayed, talked sorrowfully, filled with deep pity.

“तब वह कुन्तीपुत्र अर्जुन उन सभी बंधुओं को समरांगण में देख अत्यन्त कारुनाविष्ट हो गया और विषाद करता हुआ यों बोला I”

Thus, shown by Krishna, Arjuna recognised in his enemy lines, all his kith and kin, near and dear family members, brothers and cousins, teachers and grandsires and almost all his acquaintances and friends. He recognised such intimate relations not only in the lines, but even in his army. This sight, perhaps, brought his mind for the first time, the full realisation of the tragedies of a fratricidal war. As a warrior and a man of action, he did not perhaps until then, fully realise the extent of the sacrifice that society would be called upon to make so that his ambition might be fulfilled and Duryodhana's cruelties avenged.

Arjuna's Dilemma

Whatever might have been the cause, the sight brought into his mind a flood of pity and compassion.

Arjuna said:

28. Seeing these, my kinsmen, O Krishna, arrayed, eager to fight,
29. My limbs fail and my mouth is parched, my body quivers, and my hair stands on end.
30. The *Gandiva*-bow slips from my hand, and my skin burns all over; I am also unable to stand, and my mind is whirling round, as it were.

"अर्जुन बोला – हे कृष्ण! इन स्वजनों को युद्ध करने की इच्छा से यहा समुपस्थित देख कर मेरे अंग-प्रत्यंग शिथिल हुए जा रहे है और मुह सुखा जा रहा है I मेरा शरीर काप रहा है तथा मुझे रोमांच हो रहा है I हाथ से गाण्डीव धनुष फिसला जा रहा है I में खड़े रहने में भी समर्थ नही हु I मेरा मन चक्कर खा रहा है और हे केशव ! में चारों और अपशकुन ही देख रहा हु I"

31. And I see adverse omen, O Keshava, nor do I see my good in killing my kinsmen in battle.

हे कृष्ण! युद्ध में स्वजनों का वध करके में कोई कल्याण नही देखता I”

In these stanzas, there is an exhaustive enumeration of the symptoms that the patient could then recognise in his own physical body as a result of his mental confusions. The Sanjaya has glorified as ‘pity’, when coming out of Arjuna’s mouth, gains a more realistic expression. Arjuna says, “seeing my kinsmen gathered here anxiously determined to fight, my limbs shiver,” etc.

All these symptoms are described in the textbooks of modern psychology as typical symptoms of mental disease named ‘anxiety-neurosis’. He anxiously expected to win pleasures for himself and his relations. But the challenging look of the mighty *Kaurava* forces and the great and eminent warriors standing ready to fight, shattered his hopes, blasted his ambitions and undermined his self-confidence, and he slowly developed the well-known ‘Arjuna-disease’, the cure for which is the theme of the *Geeta.*

32. For, I desire not victory, O Krishna, nor kingdom, nor pleasures of what avail, is dominion to us, O Govinda? Of what avail are pleasures or even life itself?

"मुझे विजय नही चहिए, राज्य भी नही चाहिए I मुझे सुख की कोई इच्छा नही है I हे गोविन्द! भला राज्य से हमें क्या करना है ? भोगों से हमें क्या लेना-देना है? जीवन से ही भला हमारा क्या प्रयोजन है?"

33. They for whose sake we desire the kingdom, enjoyment, and pleasures stand here in battle, having renounced life and wealth.

34. Teachers, fathers, sons and also grandfathers, maternal uncles, fathers-in-law, grandsons, brothers-in-law and other relatives.

"हम जिनके लिए राज्य, भोग सुख आदि कि इच्छा करते है, वे ये हमारे गुरु, ताऊ, चाचा, लड़के, दादा, मामा, ससुर, पोते, साले, और अन्य सम्बधी जन अपने धन और प्राणों को त्यागकर युद्ध में खड़े है I"

35. These I do not wish to kill; they may kill me, O Madhusudhana, even for the sake of domination over the three worlds; how much less for the sake of the earth.

"हे मधुसुदन! मै इन सम्बन्धियों के द्वारा मारा जाकर भी त्रिलोकी का राज्य पाने के लिए भी इन्हें मारना नही चाहता, फिर इस प्रथ्वी के लिए क्या बात है I"

Arjuna continues his arguments to Krishna against the advisability of such a civil war between the two factions of the same royal family. A *Dharma*-hunting Arjuna is here mentally manufacturing a case for himself, justifying his cowardly retreat from the post of duty where destiny has called upon him to act.

Feeling that he had not expressed his case strongly enough to Krishna, to make him come to this conclusion, and assuming that it was because of this that the Lord had not given his assent to it, Arjuna therefore, decided to declare with a mock spirit of renunciation, that he had so much large-kill him. The climax came when Arjuna, with quixotic exaggeration, declared that he would not fight the war, even if he were to win all the three worlds of the universe, much less so for the mere Hastinapur kingship.

Arjuna's Grief

36. Killing these sons of Dhritarashtra, what pleasure can be ours, O Janardhana? Sin alone will be our gain by killing these felons.

> "हे जनार्दन I ध्रतराष्ट्र के पुत्रों को मारकर हमें भला क्या सुख मिलेगा?
> उलटे इन आततायियों को मारकर हमें पाप ही हाथ लगेगा I"

37. Therefore, we shall not kill the sons of Dhritarashtra, our relatives; for how can we be happy by killing our own people, O Madhava?

"अतएव हे माधव! अपने कुटुम्बी ध्रतराष्ट्र-पुत्रों को मारना हमे उचित नही है, क्योंकि अपने स्वजनों को मारकर हम कैसे सुखी होंगे ?"

Arjuna explains to Krishna that no good can arise out of killing the sons of Dhitarashtra. Arjuna is rounding up his arguments and coming to the dangerous conclusion that he should not kill the aggressors, nor face their heartless challenge! With the familiarity born out of his long-standing friendship, Arjuna addresses his charioteer with affection as Madhava, and asks him how one can come to any happiness after one has destroyed one's own kinsmen; still, Krishna remains silent.

38. Though these, with their intelligence clouded by greed, see no evil in the destruction of the families in the society, and no sin in their cruelty to friends.

39. Why should we not, who see evil in the destruction of the family-units, learn to turn away from this sin, O Janardhana?

"भले ही लोभ से बुद्धिभ्रष्ट हुए ये कौरवजन कुल के नाश से उत्पन्न होनेवाले दोष को तथा मित्रों से द्रोह करने के फलस्वरूप उपजनेवाले पाप को नही देख रहे है, तो भी हे जनार्दन! कुलक्षय से होनेवाले दोष को अच्छी तरह से जाननेवाले हम लोगों का पाप से बचने का उपाय क्यों नही खोजना चाहिए?"

No doubt, the *Kauravas,* grown blind in their greed for power and wealth, cannot see the destruction of the entire social structure by this war. Their ambition has so completely clouded their intelligence and sensibility that they fail to appreciate or understand the cruelty in annihilating their own friends. "If Duryodhana and his friends are behaving as blind aggressors, should the *Pandavas* not retire quietly and suffer the ignominy of a defeat and consider it their dutiful offering at the altar of peace?"

40. In the destruction of a family, the immemorial religious rites of that family perish; on the destruction of spirituality, impiety overcomes the whole family.

"कुल का नाश होने से सनातन कुल-धर्म नष्ट हो जाते है और धर्म के नष्ट होने पर फिर समूचे कुल को अधर्म दबा लेता है I"

41. By the prevalence of impiety (lack of piety), O Krishna, the women of the family become corrupt; and women being corrupted, O descendant of the *Vrishni* clan, there arises 'intermingling of castes' (*Varna-Samkara).*

"हे कृष्ण! अधर्म से दब जाने पर कुल की स्त्रिया दुषिद हो जाती है और हे वार्ष्णेय ! स्त्रियों के इस प्रकार दुषिद हो जाने पर उनके वर्णसंकरता उत्पन्न होती है I"

42. 'Confusion of castes' leads the slayer of the family to hell; for their forefathers fall, deprived of the offering of *PINDA* (rice-ball) and water (libations).

"वह वर्णसंकरता उन कुलघातियों और कुल के लिए नरक का ही कारन बनती है, क्योंकि उनके पितर लोग पिण्ड-दर्पण आदि क्रियाओं के लुप्त हो जाने से पतित हो जाते है I"

Just as a storyteller comes to add new details each time he narrates the same old story, so too, Arjuna seems to draw new inspiration from his foolishness, and each time his creative intelligence puts forth fresh arguments in support of his wrong philosophy. As soon as he finishes a stanza, he gets, as it were, a new lease of arguments to prattle (foolish talk), and takes refuge behind their noise. He indicates here that, when an individual family is destroyed, along with them the religious traditions of the society will also end, and soon an era of impiety will be ushered in.

In the largest scope of its implication, when we understand the caste system, it is the same as today's professional groups. Therefore, when they talk so seriously about the inadvisability of 'admixture of the castes, they only mean what we already know to be true in our own social pattern. An engineer in charge of a hospital and working in the operation theatre as a doctor would be a social danger, as much as a doctor would be if he is appointed as an officer for planning, guiding and executing a hydroelectric scheme!

When the general morality of society decayed, the young men and women, blinded by uncontrolled passion, start mingling without restraint. And lust knows no logic and cares least for better evolution or better culture. There will be, thereafter, unhealthy intermingling of incompatible cultural traits. The arguments are still continuing, and Arjuna points out the consequences of 'caste-admixture.' When confusion of the castes has taken place, both outside in the moral life of true discipline and one's temperament, then the family tradition gets flouted and ruined.

43. By these evil deeds of the 'destroyers of the family,' which confuse castes, the eternal religious rites of the caste and the family are destroyed.

> "(इस प्रकार) वर्णसंकरता को उत्पन्न करनेवाले उपयुक्त दोषों से उन कुल-घातीयों के सनातन कुलधर्म और जातिधर्म नष्ट हो जाते है I"

44. We have heard that, O Janardhana, it is inevitable for those men, in whose families the religious practices have been destroyed, to dwell in hell for an unknown period of time.

> "हे जनार्दन! जिनके कुलधर्म नष्ट हो चुके है ऐसे मनुष्यों का निस्संदेह नरक में वास होता है, ऐसा हमने सुना है I"

What was said in the discourse upon the earlier verse will become amply clear by the statement of Arjuna. Here also bemoaned that as a result of the civil war, the religious traditions of the families will be lost. Krishna still refuses to speak. Arjuna has come to a point where he can neither stop talking nor find any more arguments. Strangely compelling is the grace of the Lord's dignified silence. Here, Arjuna almost concludes his arguments and mentions the tradition which he had heard, that "men whose family-religion has broken down will go to hell".

45. Alas! We are involved in a great sin, in that we are prepared to kill our kinsmen, from greed for the pleasures of the kingdom.

"अहो I कितने दुःख की बात है कि हम लोग बड़ा भारी पाप करने का निश्चय कर बैठे है, जो कि इस तुच्छ राज्य-सुख के लोभ से अपने कुटुम्ब का नाश करने के लिए तैयार हो गये है I"

46. If the sons of Dhritarashtra, weapons in hand, slay me in battle, unresisting and unarmed, that would be better for me.

"यदि मुझ निहत्थे और सामना न करनेवाले को ये शस्त्रधारी धर्तराष्ट्र-पुत्र रण में मार डाले, तो वह मेरे लिए अधिक कल्याणकारी रहेगा!"

Though pitiable, it is indeed pleasantly unreasonable to watch Arjuna's intellectual exhaustion and emotional weariness as expressed. These words clearly show that instead of becoming a master of the situation, Arjuna is now a victim of it. He does not have the confidence that he is the master of the circumstances, and therefore, with a creeping sense of growing inner cowardice, he feels almost helpless, persecuted. Arjuna declares his FINAL opinion that, under the circumstances narrated during his long-drawn arguments, he should die in battle unresisting and unarmed, even if the *Kauravas* were to shoot him down, like a hunted deer, with a dozen arrows piercing his royal body.

Arjuna's Resolve

47 Having thus spoken amid the battlefield, Arjuna sat down on the seat of the chariot, casting away his bow and arrow, with a mind distressed with sorrow.

> "संजय बोला – (राजन!) उस रणभूमि में अर्जुन इस प्रकार कहकर बाणों सहित धनुष को छोड़ शोकाकुल-चित हो रथ के पिछले भाग में बैठ गया I"

The concluding stanza of this chapter contains the words of Sanjaya, in which he gives the running commentary of what he saw on the battlefield. Exhausted by his weary arguments, Arjuna, completely shattered within, sank back on the flag-staff in the open chariot, throwing down his kingly weapons.

This is the sense at which we shall leave Arjuna in the first chapter of the *Geeta.*

Chapter - 2

Yoga Of Knowledge

As discussed in the previous chapter, both the armies *Kaurvas* and *Pandvas* were ready to fight but Arjuna's emotions completely overttook his knowledge about the *Kshytriya Dharma* and he decided not to fight. This state of mind happens with most of the common people. If a loved one dies suddenly then the emotions overtake the right thinking of a person and make so many promises but when the emotions die then one realizes the reality. The same thing happened to Arjuna also. In such situations, a true friend or true well-wisher can give correct guidance, and similar is the case for Arjuna also. His friend and mentor, Krishna, gets angry and asks him to get up and fight. Krishna tells him about the duties from the Vedas and Puranas. Maharshi Vyasa has compiled it very nicely in the Bhagwat-*Geeta*. He gives the path-of-perfection sketched out in Vedas, namely, *Gyana* (ज्ञान), *Bhakti* (भक्ति), *Karma* (कर्म) and *Sannyasa* (संन्यास), paths by which Upanishada's realisation is reached. People during that period believed that these were irreconcilable factors, and so many schools of thought rose up and each started quarrelling with each other. The main emphasis during that period was an *Yagya* (यज्ञ), where sacrificing things like wood, oil, Ghee or food to please the Gods. Even sacrificing animals or any living beings in the fire was a common practice in the Vedic period. Lord Krishna used *Yagya* (यज्ञ) for sacrificing the work (कर्मा) to the Almighty or it is defined as *Nishkam-Karmas* for the *Yagya* (यज्ञ). This was a chaotic condition in which Vyasa found Hinduism during the Puranic age. In *Geeta*, Vyasa has tried to find reconciliation and a synthesis in which all the above paths can walk hand in hand, which is described by Lord Krishna to his friend, Arjuna.

The basic principles laid down in this chapter have been expanded in subsequent chapters. Overall, this chapter gives an abstract of the Bhagwat-*Geeta.* This chapter can be divided into the main five parts;

Part 1: stanzas 1-10: Lord Krishna warns Arjuna with a deep regret that he expressed on seeing the two armies arrayed against each other.

Part 2: stanzas 11-30: The Lord explains the necessity of facing the enemy according to the tenets of Sankhya-Yoga of knowledge (Yoga of logic).

Part 3: stanzas 31-38: The Lord urges Arjuna to fight the enemy because of his *Kshatriya-Dharma* which is his duty to do so.

Part 4: stanzas 39-53: The Lord explains the *Karma-Yoga* (the Yoga of selfless action) to Arjuna and tells him that if he performs his actions with a sense of duty and without attachment to the consequences, he would not incur any sin.

Part 5: stanzas 54-74: The Lord describes the qualities of a harmonised individual and the peace and tranquillity that such a Sage (Saint) enjoys.

Lord Krishna's warning to Arjuna

Lord Krishna said:

1. To him who thus was overcome with pity and despondency, with eyes full of tears and agitated, Madusudana spoke these words.

> "संजय बोले – इस तरह आसू-भरे कातर नेत्रों से युक्त करुना से घिरे हुए उस शोकातुर अर्जुन से भगवान मधुसुदन यह वचन कहने लगे I"

2. Where has this condition come upon thee, this dejection, *Un-Aryan*-like heaven-excluding, disgraceful? O Arjuna?

> "भगवान बोले – हे अर्जुन, ऐसे विषय समय में यह आर्यो को शोभा न देनेवाला, स्वर्ग का विरोधी और अपकीर्ति करनेवाला मोह तुझमे कहा से आ गया?"

3. Yield not to impotence, O *Partha,* It does not befit thee, cast off this mean weakness of heart! Stand up, O Parantapa (O scorcher of foes)!

"हे पार्थ, नपुसकता को मत प्राप्त हो; यह तुझमे शोभा नही देती I हे परन्तापन, हृद्य की इस शुद्र दुर्बलता को त्याग कर खड़ा हो I"

Lord Krishna said to Arjuna, overwhelmed by the emotion of misplaced pity and tearless weeping, Lord spoke the following words. Here, it is to be noted that modern psychology has also observed and recorded that tearless weeping is the climax of an attack of hysteria (uncontrollable emotions). Krishna, who was silent so far, is now bursting forth, in which every word is a chosen missile, a hammer stroke that can flatten any victim and told him not to yield to impotence. In modern parlance, sometimes friends wonder at the impotency of another friend and express their surprise with such an explanation as "Is he a man or a woman?," indicating that from his behaviour it is not easy to decide which character is predominant in him. Krishna also calls him an un-*Aryan* who is extremely sensitive to the higher calls of life, righteousness and nobility, both in thought and action. The soul identifies with the mind; it needs the help and guidance of the Lord or a friend. Soft words of sympathy could not have revived Arjuna's drooping mind to vigour. Thus, Krishna rightly lashed out at his friend with these stinking words. Krishna ends his word-treatments with an appeal to Arjuna to "Get up and act."

Arjuna said:

4. O Madhusudana, how shall I fight with Bhishma and Drona with arrows in the battlefield? Because O Krishna, both of them are worthy of reverence.

"अर्जुन बोला - हे मधुसुदन, रणभूमि में पितामह भीष्म और गुरु द्रौण के साथ में किस प्रकार बानो से युद्ध कर सकुगा? क्योकि हे केशवा, वे दोनों ही तो पूजा के पात्र है I"

5. It is better to live by begging than to kill these great souls, even though they are economically dependent (upon Duryodhana), my enjoyment of wealth and desire in this world would be blood of stained.

"ऐसे महात्मा और पूज्य गुरुजनों को मारने के बदले इस जगत में भीख माँगकर खाना भी निसंदेह श्रेयष्कर है, क्योकि गुरुजनों को मारकर इस संसार में आखिर उनके रक्त में सने हुए ही अर्थ और कामरूप भोगो को तो भोगुगा I"

6. We do not know which is better for us-to fight or not to fight. Nor do we know whether we will win or whether they will win. By killing those whom we have no desire to live with, those very sons of Dhritarashtra are arrayed against us.

"फिर हम यह भी तो नही जानते कि हमारे लिए क्या करना श्रेयस्कर होगा I (पता नही इस युद्ध में) हम जीतेगे या हमे वे जीत लेगे I जिन्हें मारकर हम जीना नही चाहते, वे ही ध्रतराष्ट्र-पुत्र हमारे सामने खड़े है I"

7. Therefore, overcome by ignoble feelings and confused about my duty. I beg you to show me the way which is definitely better for me. I am your disciple, I take refuge in you. Please instruct me.

“मेरा स्वभाव कायरतारूप दोष से सन गया है और धर्म का निर्णय करने में मोहितचित हो गया है I अन्त आपसे पूछता हु, जो मेरे लिए हितकर बात हो वह निश्चित रूप से मुझे बतलाए I में आपका शिष्य हु, आपकी शरण में आये हुए मुझ दास को उपदेश दीजिए I”

8. Because, even if I gain complete sovereignty over this land free from all enemies, a prosperous kingdom or supremacy over gods. I do not see any means which can alleviate the sorrow that has numbed my senses.

“क्योंकि इस प्रथ्वी निष्कंटक धन-धान्य-संपन्न राज को या देवताओ के स्वामित्व को पाकर भी मै ऐसा कोई उपाय नही देख रहा हु, जो मेरी इन्द्रियों को सुखानेवाला शोक को दूर कर सके I”

Continuing his high - sounding but futile arguments, due to his false estimates of himself and his problem, Arjuna poses here as a martyr of his own mortality and ethical goodness. Arjuna’s guru’s meaning both Drona and Bhishma, are characterised here as *Mahanubhava*-men (महानुभव) who were the ideals of their age, symbolising the best in our culture, who, in their broad-mindedness and courage of conviction, had themselves offered many sacrifices at the altars of *Dharma,* the Hindu science of perfect living. Such noble men, who formed the very touchstones of our culture in that era, were not to be eliminated from life merely for the fulfilment of the individual's appetite for power and position. Not only in their age, but for the future millennia, the world would be impoverished by the heartless squandering of such precious lives.

Thus, Arjuna says that it would be nobler for himself and the *Pandava* brothers to live upon the bread of beggary than to gain kingship after destroying all the glorious flowers in the garden of culture After killing them all, elders and teachers, even supposing the *Pandavas* got their kingdom back, Arjuna points out how his noble *Aryan*-heart would neither be able to enjoy the kingdom nor its wealth; for everything would be smeared with the bitter memories of the precious blood that would have been shed in the war.

Once we misread a situation, sentiments cloud our understanding, and then we too act like Arjuna in our life. The mind generally functions as an efficient 'receiving-dispatching clerk'. It receives the information of the perceptions conveyed to it by the sense organs. After the mind arranges the perceptions in order, it conveys them to the intellect for its judgments. The intellect, with reference to its stored-up information of similar experiences in the past, comes to find the final judgements. They are conveyed to the mind for execution, and the mind, in its turn, issues the necessary orders for the organ of action to act upon. All these activities are happening at every moment, throughout our walking state, in our intelligent existence, amid the objects of the world, and therefore, Arjuna is seen here as being incapable of judging whether he should conquer his enemy or, by an ignoble (purpose) retreat, allow them to conquer him.

When Arjuna has completely realised the helpless impotency within himself to come to any decision, he surrenders totally to Krishna. In his own words, he admits the psychological shattering felt and lived by him in his bosom. He has instinctively and correctly diagnosed the cause of it to be 'an uncontrollable amount of overcoming pity'. Of course, Arjuna does not realise that it is his misplaced compassion; whatever may be the patient is now under the mental stress of extreme confusion and bewilderment. Arjuna confesses that his intellect is obstructed by a cloud of confusion regarding what *Dharma* (धर्म) and *Adharma* (अधर्म) are at that moment for him. The problem of whether to fight and conquer the enemies or not to fight and allow the enemies to conquer him, which needed an urgent solution, could not be rationally judged with the depleted mental capacities of Arjuna.

Arjuna is indicating here to Krishna the urgency of guidance, but for which he would be left to suffer the voiceless agonies of an inward pain. The mental sorrow in Arjuna is blasting even his sense-organs under the heavy burden of his sorrows; he finds it very difficult even to see or hear things properly. Even his sense organs are blasted by the overheated sorrows within him.

The urgency felt by Arjuna, as is evident from his own words, may be considered as amounting to his burning aspirations for liberating himself. All that he needed to make himself perfect was right-discrimination (विवेक), which the Lord of senses (Harikrishna) gives him throughout the Divine songs.

Sanjaya said:

9. O king, after Gudakesha (Arjuna), the conqueror of his enemies, had spoken thus to Harikesha, (Krishna), he said to Govinda (Krishna), "I shall not fight" and became silent.

"संजय बोला - हे शत्रुतापन ध्रतराष्ट्र, निद्राविजयी अर्जुन अंतरयामी भगवान कृष्ण से इस प्रकार कह चुकने के बाद साफ-साफ यह बात कहकर कि मै युद्ध नही करूँगा, चुप हो गया I"

10. O Bharata (Dhritrashtra), then Harikesha, smiling as it were, spoke these words to Arjuna, who was sitting dejected between the two armies.

"हे भरत, इस तरह दोनों सेनाओ के बीच शोक करते हुए अर्जुन से भगवान श्रीकृष्ण मुसकराते हुए – उसे यह वचन कहने लगे I"

This constitutes the running commentary of Sanjaya - the faithful reporter of the *Geeta* to Dhritarashtra. He says that after surrendering himself (Arjuna) to Krishna and seeking the Lord's guidance, he sat down and said he would not fight and then became silent.

No single individual alive during that period of time had the authority to call back the armies from the field of Kurukshetra, except the blind old uncle of the *Pandavas.* He had the necessary status and weight of opinion for ordering a truce even at a time when it looked as though the time had slipped through his fingers. Sanjaya hoped that Dhritarashtra would understand the futility of their fighting against Arjuna, who would certainly conquer the *Kavrava* forces. But Dhritarashtra was born blind, and had grown deaf to the words of warning uttered by the good people, due to the infinite attachment (मोह) to his children. Further, Sanjaya narrated to his king that, standing between two forces (the good and bad), arrayed for a battle of death, Arjuna (The Jeeva, जीव) surrendered completely to the Lord, his charioteer. The Lord, with a smile, reassures the Jeeva (Arjuna) of its final victory, and declares the entire message of spiritual redemption, the *Geeta.* The charioteer (the pure intellect) would lend to the ego a divine strength, and guide it to the ultimate victory over the forces of *Adharama* (अधर्म), with the help of the dynamism of *Dharma* (धर्म), even though the former may seem much stronger in force than the simple-looking dynamism in the latter.

Necessity of Facing the Enemy

The Lord said:

11. You have grieved for those that should not be grieved for, yet, you speak words of wisdom. The wise grieve neither for the living nor the dead.

> "भगवान बोले – जिनके लिए शोक करना उचित नही, उनके लिए तू शोक कर रहा है और साथ ही ज्ञान की बड़ी – बड़ी बाते भी बोला जा रहा है, परन्तु जो यथार्थ में ज्ञानीजन होते है, वे न तो उनके लिए शोक करते है जिनके प्राण चले गये है और न उनके लिए ही जिनके प्राण नहीं गयें है I"

The real teaching of the Bhagwat-*Geeta* starts from this shloka. Does it mean whatever is told in Chapter 1, and in previous Shlokas not useful? No, the background told in the *Mahabharta* and in the previous chapter is important for further understanding of Lord Krishna's teachings. As mentioned in the previous section, Arjuna says he will not fight the war and wants to become a *Sannyasi* (संन्यासी) and the reason is attachment (मोह) with the near and dear ones. To justify his arguments, he gave many reasons like killing relatives and many innocent people and accruing sin, killing his own teacher (Guru), a god like grandfather, Bhishma Pitamah and respected members. He (Arjuna) had ignored the overall situation of how the war was started. And at the last moment, the attachment overtook and decided not to fight.

An important word appears in the shloka, a man-of-wisdom (ज्ञानी), which means a man who thinks from the inner-consciousness for any problem or situation. Adi Shankaracharyya defined such a person as a *Brahman or Pandith* who always thinks from self-consciousness and not from material-consciousness. Are Bhishma, Dhrona, etc. *Gyanis or Brahman*? Yes, they are the man-of-wisdom (ज्ञानिस), but they are bound by their duties, such as Bhishma's oath to protect the throne. He does not have any say in whether any injustice is happening in the kingdom. He can suggest the king but cannot disobey the king. Similar is the case with Dhronacharyya and Kripacharyya, *Dharm*-Guru of the Hastinapur kingdom. Do these intellectuals (ज्ञानि) justify supporting such a king who is immoral and not good for the masses? We feel it is not justified, and at least they can abstain from taking part in such a war, despite their oath.

So far, Lord Krishna has not argued with Arjuna. He (Krishna) has listened to it very carefully and realised that Arjuna has a deep-rooted attachment (मोह). His disease (मोह) cannot be removed easily, and to eradicate his disease, he has to be told the ETERNAL REALITY. Now he tells Arjuna that a man of wisdom (ज्ञानी) neither feels sorry nor happy for dead or alive people. Because he knows one day one has to die, and he (ज्ञानी) knows that all are living, according to their own nature (प्रकृति). He (ज्ञानी) knows that the nature or *Prakriti* is formed according to their own *Karmas* (actions). Even a man of wisdom works according to his own *Prakriti*. Lord

Krishna tells Arjuna that a man of consciousness (विवेक) should not feel sorry for the dead or alive.

Krishna is advising Arjuna to renounce his physical emotions and intellectual estimates of his teacher, Dhrona and his grandsire, Bhishma and those of the whole battlefield problem and to re-evaluate the situation through his spiritual understanding.

Arjuna analysed Krishna's arguments and thought he was not only worried about Dhronachrayya and Bhishma but also for other kings who had come for the war. He says, Do you mean we should not feel sorry for the other kings also?

At every level of our personality, we view life and come to our own conclusions about things. Thus, we have a physical estimate of the world from the body level, which is quite distinct from the REALITY of life from mental and also intellectual concepts of life that are from the level of inner-consciousness

When we rightly diagnose Arjuna's dejection, it is not very difficult for us to realise that through immediate cause is the challenge of the war, his condition of mental torture is only a symptom of a deeper disease. Just as a true doctor will eradicate a disease, not by curing the symptoms but by removing the cause of the disease, so too here, Lord Krishna is trying to remove the very source of Arjuna's delusion.

Reincarnation Theory

"Why do they deserve no grief?" It is because they are eternal- and how is it so? The Lord says in the following stanza.

12. It is not that, at any time in the past, I was not or when you or these kings were not; nor is it that we shall not be in the future.

'मैं किसी काल मे नही था ऐसा नही, तू कभी नही था ऐसा नही, ये राजा लोग कभी नही थे ऐसा भी नही, और इसके बाद भी हम सब न होगे ऐसा भी नही है (अर्थात् हम पहलें भी थे, इस समय है और आगे भी होगे I"

Krishna here declares in unequivocal terms that the embodied soul in everyone is set on a great pilgrimage in which it comes to identify itself with varied forms temporarily to gain a limited but determined set of experiences. He says that neither he, nor Arjuna, nor the great kings of the ages that have assembled in both armies are mere accidental happenings. They do not come from nowhere and, at their death, do not become mere non-existent nothingness. Correct philosophical thinking guides man's intellect to the apprehension of a continuity from the past through the present to the endless future. The self (आत्मा) remains the same, it gets seemingly conditioned (spirit) by the different body-equipment and comes to live through its self-ordered environments. The almighty (ईश्वर) is always present in the past, present and future. The *Atama* (self) is the part of *Ishwara* (Almighty), also remains the same; it gets seemingly conditioned by different body-equipments and comes to live through its self-ordained environments. When the body-equipment (life) goes or dies, the self *(Atama)*, along with the soul, remains and finds another body-equipment (life), depending upon the present spirit (*Karmas*).

It is this conclusion of the Vedic philosophers that has given us the most satisfactory theory of REINCARNATION. The most powerful opponents of this idea do not seem to have followed their scriptures. Christ Himself has, if not directly, at least indirectly, proclaimed this doctrine when He told His disciples, John the origin who was the most learned of the Christian Fathers, has clearly declared "Every man received a body for himself according to his desires (*Karmas*) in former lives."

There was no great thinker in the past who had not, or in the present who has not accepted, expressly these logical conclusions about the DOCTRINE OF REINCARNATION. Buddha constantly made references to his previous births. Virgil and Ovid regarded the doctrine as perfectly self-evident. Josephas observed that the belief in reincarnation was widely accepted among the Jews of his era. Solomon's book of wisdom says, "To be born in a sound mind with a sound body is a reward of the virtues of the past lives."

And who does not remember the famous saying of the learned son of Islam who declared, "I died out of the plant and became an animal; I died out of an animal and became a man. Why, then do I fear to die? When did I grow less by dying? I shall die out of man and shall become an angel."

In later times, this most intelligent philosophical belief has been accepted as a doctrine by the German philosophers, Goethe, Fichte, Schelling and Lessing. Among the recent philosophers Hume, Spencer, and Max Muller have recognised this doctrine as incontrovertible. Among the poets of the West, we also find many burnished intellectuals soaring into the cloudless sky of imagination. Within their poetic flights, they, too, have intuitively felt the sanction behind this immortal doctrine–Browning, Rossetti, Tennyson and Wordsworth, to mention a few names.

The REINCARNATION THEORY is not to mean the dream of philosophers and the day is not far off, when with fast developing science of psychology, the West will come to rewrite its scriptures under sheer weight of observed phenomenon. Science has made great progress in spirituality due to quantum physics and Nanoscience. Recently, scientists have got a definite clue that there is a link between past, present and future for a certain time due to the quantum effect (htts: youtube | 8Y4K6TJOPUK) which supports the theory of reincarnation mentioned in Vedas. An uncompromising intellectual quest for understanding life cannot satisfy itself if it is thwarted at every corner by 'observing irregularities.' We cannot for long ignore them all as mere 'chances.' The prodigy Mozart is a spectacular instance, which cannot be explained to be logical; we must accept the idea of the continuity of the embodied souls. This genius wrote Sonatas at the age of four, played in public at the age of five, and composed his first opera at the age of seven. Without the Reincarnation theory, we will have to leave this wonderful incident an accident, and throw it into the dustbin by chance, and bury it there. Many examples are often noticed in India also, but rarely recorded as evidence to prove the great reincarnation theory. The modern world has yet to discover this great self-evident LAW OF LIFE. Therefore, to an uninitiated student, this theory may seem too staggering for quiet appreciation.

Krishna declared to Arjuna that "none of them (including himself, Arjuna and the great kings) even after their deaths on the battlefield shall cease to exist in future", Arjuna, who was a typical man-of-the-world, could not grasp it as a self-evident fact. His (Arjuna's) questioning eyes made the Lord explain this idea again through an example, "Why do they deserve no grief?" for they are eternal. How? The Lord says:

13. Just as in this body the embodied (*Atama*) passes into childhood, youth and old age, so also does he pass into another body; the firm man does not grieve at it.

"देहधारी (स्थूल-शरीर) को इस देह में जिस प्रकार बालपन, तरूनाई और बुढ़ापा प्राप्त होता है, उसी प्रकार (आगे उसी आत्मा को) दूसरे देह की प्राप्ति होती हैI अत: इस विषय में ज्ञानी पुरुष मोहित नही होता I"

In the previous shloka, the Lord convinced Arjuna why he should not worry about the death of his near and dear and the kings, gathered on the battlefield, because the self *(Atama)* cannot be killed. Arjuna got convinced, but again he says it is natural when the body of a near and dear one is killed, one feels sorry for it. Again, the Lord says to Arjuna that he should not worry about when the body is dead because when childhood is dead, the youthful is born, and when youth is dead, the oldness is born. Therefore, he says we don't worry when the youthness is dead; on the other hand, we feel happy because we get a lot of experience in old age. Similarly, when oldness is dead (death), the embodied soul gets a new body to fulfil the experiences left in the previous body. Therefore, Krishna tells him that a man of wisdom (ज्ञानी-पुरुष) does not worry about the death of an embodiment. But for the common people, death is sudden, so it is a sad or sorry situation. However, from childhood to youth and then to adulthood or from adulthood to old age is a continuous change and slow process so we don't feel sad. The continuous change is nature's law (प्रकृति).

Here, it is better to explain some points regarding the soul and self (*Atama*) for common people. Life is the combination of imperishable soul (सूक्ष्म-शरीर) and perishable materialistic body (स्थूल-शरीर). The soul consists of self (आत्मा) and spirit (देहि-आत्मा). The materialistic body consists of mind, intelligence, sense-organs, action organs, etc., which are perishable. The spirit has a direct link with the materialistic mind and imperishable *Atama* (self). All materialistic impressions *(Karmas)* are coated in the spirit. The soul responsible for the rebirth means the spirit of the previous births.

This stanza is again asserting in unequivocal terms the truth behind the reincarnation theory. And thus viewed, the death of childhood, following which alone, we can come to experience youth. We are confident in our knowledge that though the youth is entered into and childhood has ended, there is a continuity of on every moment of death, there is no extinction of the individuality, but the embodied-ego (soul) of the dead body leaves its previous structure, and according to the *Vasanas* (spirit or mental impressions) that it had gathered during its embodiment, it gets identified with a physical equipment, where it can express itself completely and seeks its fulfilment. The previous life experiences he cannot remember because the new body mental equipment is totally different. However, the soul is the same in the new body, which affects the overall behaviour of the new body. Sometimes, with our best efforts, we fail or get unexpected results because of the previous life impressions on the soul, which we call it as fate or luck.

Lord Krishna further says that the human's materialistic body is continuously in change from birth to death, but there is a constant factor in him due to which we remember right from childhood to old age, and that constant factor is called the soul, consisting of the self (*Atama*) and the spirit. A man who knows the functions of body and soul is called a man of wisdom (ज्ञानी). Krishna further tells him to become a man of wisdom, but it takes dedication and a lot of time, until that time we feel the sorrow for the death of near and dear. Lord Krishna clarifies this question to Arjuna in the following Shloka.

14. O Kaunteya (Arjuna), cold and heat, pleasure and pain, which arise through the interaction of the senses and the sense organs, are impermanent as they come and go. Therefore, O Bharata (Arjuna), patiently endure them.

> "हे कुन्तीपुत्र, इन्द्रियों और उनके साथ विषयों के सन्योग शीत – उष्ण, सुख-दु:ख आदि द्वन्दों को उपाजते है; वे आते है और चले भी जाते है, अत: अनित्य हैI इस कारन से भरतवंशी अर्जुन, उनको तू सहन कर."

Lord Krishna tells Arjuna that heat-cold and pleasure-pain etc. come and go. They are not permanent, and one should come to a normal state as quickly as possible. If a close person dies, then it is natural to feel pain, but a man who has an attachment with him may come to a normal state in months, but one should try to learn how to come to normal quickly. Here in this shloka, two examples are given: heat-cold and pleasure-pain. One has to face heat and cold boldly because we cannot control it, but that is also not permanent. However, one should try to learn how to adjust to such things. A man of knowledge has learned to adjust to keep mental equanimity for such dual qualities as he knows this duality is the quality of *Maya* (illusions). Therefore, Krishna advises Arjuna to rise above such dualities and try to learn how to keep equanimity in such conditions as they are not permanent.

The external objects can convey their stimuli and give us an experience only when our minds come in contact with the objects through the sense organs. The object cannot remain permanently, but out of necessity must pass on to become one with the entire past. Nothing can remain the same even for a short period, in the world of objects where change alone is changeless law. Having understood this finite nature of the changeable object of the world, wherein every one of them has a beginning and an end, on no occasion need a wise man despair the least of things THAT ARE, or of things THAT ARE NOT. Heat and cold, success and failure, pain or joy – none of these can be permanent. Since every situation of its own nature must keep on changing, it would be foolish of us to get upset at every change we notice. It is the attitude of the wise to go through life, both in joy and failure, in pain and joy, with constant awareness: Even this will pass away.

What good will accrue to him who is indifferent to heat and cold and the like, given in the next stanza?

15. That firm man to whom, surely, these affect not, O chief among men, to whom pleasure and pain are the same, is fit for realising the immortality of the self *(Atama)*.

"हे पुरुषश्रेष्ट I सुख-दुःख में समान रहनेवाला जिस धीर पुरुष को ये इन्द्रिया और विषयों से संयोग व्यथित नही करते, वहीं अमरता का अधिकारी होता है I"

Calm personality (nature), both in pleasure and pain, is a condition necessary for the right knowledge of the true self (*Atama*); this is the technique of self-realisation, as explained in the Upanishadic lore. Based upon this fact, Lord Krishna explains that the one who has found in himself a mental equipoise, wherein he is not afflicted or disturbed by circumstances of pain and pleasure, is fit to be called 'super-manhood'.

So long as we live in the body, as the body, we are not able to ignore or calmly endure the sorrows of the body. But when we are fired by sentiments of love or hatred, we invariably make ready sacrifices of bodily pleasures. Because of my love for my son, I am ready to make any sacrifice of my physical needs, so that I can give him a good education, etc. When one gets fired up intellectually by some idea or ideology, for the satisfaction of it, one readily ignores and overlooks the comforts and pleasures of one's body and mind. It is especially said that the equipoise of the mind, both in pleasure and pain, entertained by wise men makes him fit for the highest cultural self-development. That is to say, the equanimity should not flow from the dark caves of one's stupidity and inertia, but it must gurgle forth from the open sunny fields of wisdom and understanding. When one understands the essential nature of the objects of the world to be finite, out of the realised knowledge one gains enough balance for a calm mind, and feels neither exalted in pleasure nor dejected in pain.

For the following reasons, it is proper that you should abandon your grief and distressing delusion and should calmly endure heat and cold, etc., for:

16. The unreal (असत्य) has no existence, and the real (सत्य) is not destroyed. The truth about both these has been told by the seers.

"असत्य का कभी अस्तित्व नही होता और जो सत्य है, उसकी कभी हार नही होतीI वास्तव में तत्वद्रष्टाओ ने इन दोनों का इस प्रकार अन्तिम निश्चय किया है I"

In Vedantic literature, the Real and Un-Real are very scientifically distinguished. The *Rushis* have clearly indicated what constitutes the real and Un-Real. The unreal is that which was not in the past and which will not be in future, but that which seemingly exists only in the present. The Lord is trying to tell us through this shloka that it is difficult to understand or to know the REAL things because it cannot be known by our sense organs. Adi Shankaracharya says a special method is to be used to know this, which is called *Dhyana* yoga (ध्यान-योग) or consciousness through which one can understand the permanent basic original of the materialistic and non-materialistic world (परम-मूल-कारन).

The life in our matter envelopment (body), we know, is finite, inasmuch as very little experience, at all these levels of our existence-among the objects, with our sentiments, and in the company of our ideas, is finite. The body changes at every moment, the mind evolves, and the intellect grows. All changes, evolutionary moments, and growths are indicated by a constant death of their previous state. In order that the things concerned may change, evolve or grow. The body, the mind, and the intellect are ever changing in us, and all of them, therefore, according to our definition, cannot be the Real.

But is there any REAL entity behind it all? So that change may take place, no doubt, a changeless substratum (thing) is necessary. For the water to flow in the river, a motionless riverbed must exist. Similarly, in order to hold together the millions of experiences at the level of our body, mind and intellect, and to give us the experience of synchronised whole-which we call life, we must necessarily have some sub-stratum that is changeless and Real, It is common for three, (past, present and future) is the soul (सूक्ष्म-शरीर).

Something in us remains as it were, unchanged all through our changes, holding the vivid experiences together, just as the thread holds the beads in the necklace. On closure analyses, it becomes clear that it can be nothing other than the *Atama* (self) in us, the pure Awareness. Experiences that have come under one's awareness do not constitute any vital aspect of one's life; life is the sum total of experiences that have been devised by the touch of one's illuminating consciousness. In childhood, I was conscious of my childhood, in youth, I was conscious of my youth; and in my old age, I am again conscious of my present experiences. The consciousness remains the same, endless experiences came under it, got illuminated and died away. The awareness by which I become conscious of things in my life, because of which I am considered as alive – "THAT" spiritual entity, internal, all-pervading, un-born, un-dying, and one changeless Factor, is the Infinite in me, and this self *(Atama)* is the Real one.

Men of knowledge and wisdom have known the essence, the meaning, and the implication of both these: the self (*Atama*) and the non-self, the real and the unreal, which in their mysterious combination constitute the strange phenomenon called the world.

What then is that which is REAL?

17. Know him as an indestructible who pervades this universe. None is capable of destroying this imperishable one (*Atama* or soul).

> "तू यह जान ले कि जिनके द्वारा यह सारा जगत व्याप्त है, वह तो अविनाशी है, क्योकि इस अव्यक्त का नाश करने में, कोई भी समर्थ नही है I"

The REAL is that which envelopes everything that exists, and which is the very stuff and substance of all the worlds of perceptions, which we experience. Different mud pots, each different in form, shape and colour, may have different names according to the things they contain, or according to the purpose for which they are used. Though each of them has a different name, yet all of them are; we may say, enveloped by, or permitted with one and the same stuff, the mud, without which none of the pots exist. From mud they come, in mud they exist, and when they are destroyed, their names and forms shall merge back to become mud. All the mud-pots are enveloped by mud, which is the Reality holding the world of mud-pots together. Similarly, the world of finite (individual) changes is entirely permitted through and enveloped by the REAL; even for a moment, ever getting destroyed, even by a fraction.

Who is non-perishable, the Real, who envelopes the whole world, who keeps the world in order and sustains the world. He (Almighty) produces, sustains and destroys the un-real things. Similarly, in the living beings the consciousness remains through their birth, youth and old age and remains even after death; therefore, it is Real, which is a part of the almighty. In non-leaving beings, there is continuous change, and change is the constant in the materialistic world.

What then is the unreal (असत्य) whose existence is not constant?

18. They have an end, it is said, these bodies of the embodied-self. The self is Eternal, indestructible, and incomprehensible. Therefore, fight, O Bharata.

"नाशरहित, अमाप, नित्य, शरीरी आत्मा के ये सारे अवयव नाशवान कहे गये है I अनएव हे भरतवंशी, अर्जुन, तू युद्ध कर I"

The physical forms, constituted of matter envelopments, are all perishable equipment for the indwelling (आत्मा). This *Atama* (self) is an internal factor, ever in its nature, changeless, indestructible and imperishable. By the term ever changeless, Krishna is indicating that eternal because the non-eternals, by their nature, must be ever changing, change being the characteristic (insignia) of the finite. Here, by using two terms, Eternal (नित्य) and indestructible (अनाशिनः), the Lord is indicating that neither total nor partial destruction is possible in the supreme.

It will be useful to clarify Self *(Atama)* in detail as follows:

It is not a body part but an energy concentrated in the head, but not a head part, which we call consciousness (चेतना). The *Atama* (self) and the materialistic body cannot live separately until we are alive. The consciousness can be used in two ways. One way is for our selfishness, or body parts or attachments or egoness. Another way is for other aspects like science, politics or social work. The *Atama* or consciousness is nothing but the energy, like any other energy in science, like electrical, magnetic or nuclear or gravitational energies. The energy, we cannot make zero, but we can convert it into some other form. The electrical energy can be converted into heat, magnetic or light, etc. Similarly, the consciousness energy cannot become zero when the body or head of a human being is dead, which is the materialistic part. But the consciousness of the being is diverted to some other materialistic body, depending upon the human being's *Karmas* (past *Karmas*), influences on the energy (*Atama*). Therefore, Krishna tells Arjuna that your *Atama* (self) is never dead, but only your materialistic body dies. So, do not get attached to temporary things, so get up and fight against Bhishma and Dhronacharya.

The Lord now quotes two Vedic Mantras to confirm the view that *Geeta-Shastra* is intended to remove the cause of *Sansara* (संसार), such as grief and delusion. "It is only a false notion of yours, says the Lord, "that you think thus Bhisma and others will be killed by me (meaning Krishna or the supreme) in the battle. I (supreme) will be their slayer." How?

19. He who regards this self (आत्मा) as the destroyer of someone, or he who considers it as being killed, is both ignorant, because it neither kills nor is killed by anybody.

"इस आत्मा को जो मारनेवाला समजता है और जो उसे मारा गया मानता है, वे दोनों ही नही जानते है I यह आत्मा न तो मारता है, न मारा ही जाता है I"

20. *Atama* is neither born nor does it die at any time; nor having once existed, it ceases to be; it is unborn, eternal, everlasting, and ancient. It does not die when the body is slain.

"यह आत्मा न कभी जन्मता है और न मरता है I ऐसा नही कि यह नही होकर फिर से हो जाता है (अथवा यह भी नही कि यह होकर फिर से अभाव-रूप हो जाता है) यह आत्मा तो अजन्मा, नित्य, शास्वत और पुरातन है I वह शरीर के नष्ट होने पर नाश को नही प्राप्त होता I"

21. He who knows the self as indestructible, everlasting, unborn and unchanging, O Parth, how can that person kill or cause to be killed?

"हे अर्जुन, जो इस आत्मा को अविनाशी, नित्य, अजन्मा और अव्यय जानता है, वह पुरुष भला किसी को कैसे मार सकता है अथवा मरवा सकता है?"

The *Atama* (self) being Immutable is neither slain nor can it be the slayer. Those who think that they have been slain when the body is slain and those who feel they are the slayers are both ignorant of the real nature of the self, and hence they simply foolish assertions. That which is killed is the perishable body and the delusory arrogation; the notion 'I have killed" belongs to the ego of the person. The self is that which is beyond the body and the ego. In short, being immutable, the *Atama* (self) can neither be the agent nor the object of the action of slaying or killing. The Lord is trying to remove from Arjuna's mind the concept that killing one's near and dear is sinful. He explains that the real culprit behind sinfulness is the ego attached to one's role as the doer. When this ego of duty is dropped and one ceases to desire the fruits of action, the sinfulness of the action does not affect him. All the symptoms of mutability that are recognised and experienced by the body. The body is prone to different changes, and these changes are the source of all sorrows in every embodiment. These five changes are common to all and they may be enumerated as: birth, existence, growth, decay and death. These are the common womb of all pains in a mortal life. All these changes are denied in the *Atama* (self). Unlike the physical body, the *Atama* is not born; it is the Eternal factor that exists at all times. Waves are born and they die away, but the ocean is not born with waves; nor does it die when the waves disappear. Since there is no birth, there is no death; things that have a beginning alone can end, the rising waves alone can moan their dying conditions. Again, it is explained that like the birth of a child who was not in existence before, and who has come to exist after the birth, the *Atama* (self) is not something that has come to be born due to or because of the body. Thus, *Atama* is Unborn, Eternal, Birthless and Deathless (अजन्म, नित्य).

Analysis of self (*Atama*)

If *Atama* is *Nitya* (नित्य), the following three questions arise in anybody's mind: As the Lord says, *Atama* (self) neither can grow nor decrease nor take birth nor die, and it is everywhere and non-perishable. There would be no scope for decrease or increase if the thing has a size or shape, but the self is sizeless and shapeless and limitless. Therefore, the question of changes in *Atama* does not arise. Now the question arises, who is the killer and who is killed? When a man is killed, his materialistic body is killed, but not the self or *Atama*. Here, one more question arises: who is responsible for killing? Because the materialistic body is insentient and *Atama* does not do any action. Now the second question arises, why scriptures or in day-to-day life do we condemn or think about the sin-ness in violence or innocent killings? The third question arises if the self is actionless and the materialistic body is insentient, who does such sin-ness affect the killing or violence because the body is anyway perishable; therefore, there should not be any sin in killing it. Let us analyse these three questions together.

As we have seen above, who is killed is his materialistic body, and who kills somebody is his Ego and not by the *Atama* or the body. The ego is the product of mind, intellect and courage, which is accumulated in the soul (सुक्ष्म-शरीर). This soul consists of pure self or *Atama* and spirit. The spirit can be pure or impure (ego) depending upon the *Karmas* (actions). It is just like covering a transparent sheet around a diamond. The sheet is dirty if you have more bad *Karmas* and ego. This sheet can be made transparent by virtuous actions (*Karmas*). Consciousness comes from the soul to the mind. If one uses consciousness from the self or *Atama*, one does good actions. Therefore, it is the nature of the soul (spirit or ego) that gets affected by the duality of sin-ness or virtuous deeds and not by the materialistic body or the *Atama* (self), and because of ignorance, we feel the self or *Atama* is responsible for everything.

One more question is left out. If a man dies of natural death in young or old age, due to the vital organ failure, connected to the mind. And the mind fails, which is the central processing of the materialistic body, perishes (dies) What about the self (*Atama*), which is non-perishable? The *Atama* or self, along with the spirit (soul) or (सुक्ष्म-शरीर or लिंगधारी-शरीर), will find another body depending upon the influence of *Karmas*, accumulated in the spirit (soul) in the present and past lives.

Summarising what is said so far as the Law-of-Being (धर्म) of the *Atama* (self), which indicated rather than defined the Eternal, Immutable Reality and those who know this shall have, thereafter, no dejection or sorrow in facing life's realities. Krishna asks Arjuna, 'How can one arrogate to oneself the stupid idea of ageing? The Lord says that neither can such an individual cause someone to slay nor himself be a slayer in the context of the present war (*Mahabharata*).

In what way is the self (*Atama*) indestructible?

22. Just as a person casting off old clothes puts on new ones, in the same way, the *Atama* (self) abandons the old body and enters into a new one.

"जैसे मनुष्य फटे-पुराने कपड़ो को त्यागकर, अन्य नये कपडे पहन लेता है, वैसे ही यह शरीर आत्मा (soul) भी जीर्ण शरीरो को छोड़कर अन्य नये शरियो में प्रवेश कर जाता ह"I"

Just as an individual changes his clothes to suit the convenience of the occasion, so too the *Atama* (self) discards one physical form and takes another, which will be most suited for it to gain the next required type of experiences. Who decides what types of clothes are suitable, which is done by the Ego-centric spirit which surrounds the *Atama* (self). No one will plan to go to his office wearing his nightgown; nor will he, in his stiff collar, feel happy while playing tennis in the evening. He changes his dress according to the field where he is intending to work for the time being. Similar is the way and wherefore of the death and thereafter. In short, this is the doctrine of incarnation, which we have already explained in earlier stanzas.

On the whole, it must have definitely conveyed to Arjuna the idea that it grins only at those who have no understanding, and that it has no pain for those who understand its implications and workings. Just as changing of the dress is no pain to the body, so too, when the dweller in the body leaves the envelopment, there is no pain possible again, undressing does not mean that thereafter, we will ever live naked, so too, the embodied *Atama* along with the spirit, before long discovers an appropriate equipment from which to function, and to earn for itself new sets of experiences. Evolution and change are all for the mind and intellect and not for the *Atama* (self). The *Atama* is perfect and changeless, and needs no evolution.

Rebirth Theory in the 20th century:

If we consider that the present life is only available to us, then serious philosophical and scientific questions arise. Why do people have different behaviour? Some are born rich and some are poor, etc. Secondly, some people are very smart, some are ugly, some are healthy, and some are weak by birth itself. The second point can be explained scientifically on the basis of DNA Jeans theory in biology, but not the first one. In such cases, we wonder why God or nature or the almighty is partial to some people. But the almighty cannot be impartial, and science cannot explain this aspect. The Vedantic philosophy, supported by the Bhagwat-*Geeta*, can explain the first point on the basis of *Karma* theory. The time is not far off, scientifically also it will be proven the theory of rebirth due to tremendous advancement in computers, nanotechnology, communication, biological and medical sciences. Already we know in nano-technology that a particular nano-particle from where it has come, where it will stay (stable) and where it will go (react), supporting the theory of rebirth.

Charles Darwin's theory of evolution:

The rebirth concept, particularly in Vedantic philosophy, gives a strong indication that there is a definite aim or purpose in human life. It is not just an accidental happening for human beings like any other living beings. Earlier, nearly two centuries ago, science also, like the materialistic thought today, that life is just accidental. But today's science thinks there is a definite aim and purpose for the birth of human beings. Nearly two centuries ago, Charles Darwin of England gave a revolutionary idea of "theory of evolution" for the living beings, and there was a lot of opposition to his idea in the scientific community during that time. He studied and researched many species of living beings and came to the conclusion that all the species are tied to the evolution process. Roughly speaking following are his conclusions:

1. Life starts with a primitive living being, "Amoeba."
2. This life goes from different species and ends with human beings.
3. Life goes from one species to another for two reasons. One is survival of the fittest, and secondly, natural selection or sexual selection.

Keeping aside how one type of species evolves into another, there are many questions scientifically and philosophically. As Darwin says, life starts with Amoeba and ends with a human being. Does the evolution of life end with human beings or does it start again with Amoeba? Or is there any process of further evolution?

Secondly, is there any aim or purpose for this cycle of life process, up to human beings? As we see in the past, there are super-human beings like Buddha, Christ, Adi Shankaracharyya, Swamy Vivekananda or Saint Gyaneshwar, etc. Does it mean that evolution takes place even in human beings themselves? If humans are the highest evolved living beings, then why is there a lot of difference in the human being itself, like one is cruel and another is a saint. These questions cannot be answered by Darwin's theory nor satisfied scientifically. However, these questions can be answered very satisfactorily based on rebirth theory, given in Vedanta, based on *Karmas* although the scientific data are not available in the scientific laboratory, but with the tremendous inventions, we are confident that the rebirth theory will also be proved scientifically.

Incidents of rebirth:

Not only in India but all over the world, there are incidents where a four years old child tells about past life incidents when such incidents are confirmed to be correct. The people who do not believe in rebirth tell such incidents as an extra-sensory perception. In that case, why should it happen in such rare cases only? We strongly believe and scientifically justify that although the soul (सूक्ष्म-शरीर) is the same in previous and present life but the equipment or mind in both is not the same, which is made up of constituents in both lives (different parents). If the mind somewhat matches homogeneously in both lives, then one remembers the past life experiences in childhood. Now the question arises why the past life experiences in such cases are remembered only in childhood and not in adulthood? The soul is fresh (pure) in childhood, so the child can remember the past life incidences whereas in adulthood, the present life soul is influenced by present life incidences only. However, in adulthood also we sometimes remember past-life experiences in dreams. Such incidents make us believe there is a rebirth, mentioned in Vedanta.

Rebirth Theory - Karmic (actions)

The rebirth principle is based on the *Karma* theory, particularly for human beings. We cannot live the lives of humans in their natural flow like any other animal, as humans have intelligence. We have a lot of variations in the behaviour of humans that also cannot be explained without the Karmic theory. The present life is based on past life *Karmas* (प्रभद्र), and the present life *Karmas* decides the future birth. The intent of the *Karmas* is more important than showing off to others. For example, two people help one widowed woman. One helps with a selfish motive, and the second helps genuinely. The second person's *Karma* is considered good *Karmas*. All these good and bad *Karmas* are recorded (influenced) in the soul (spirit), which is responsible for the rebirth.

The rebirth theory can be explained by taking the resonance phenomenon in physics as follows:

Let us try to plot a graph for the rebirth principle in human beings only because humans are the highest evolved species among the living beings. Let us take the parent's womb energy on the X-axis and the dead person's soul energy on the Y-axis in Hertz (Hz). The

Tamssic womb energy is from 10-40, for *Rajssic* 30-70 and *Sattvic* 60-95. And for other living beings, it is less than 10 where their aim is struggle for existence and reproduction, where the rebirth principle can be based on Darwin's theory of evolution.

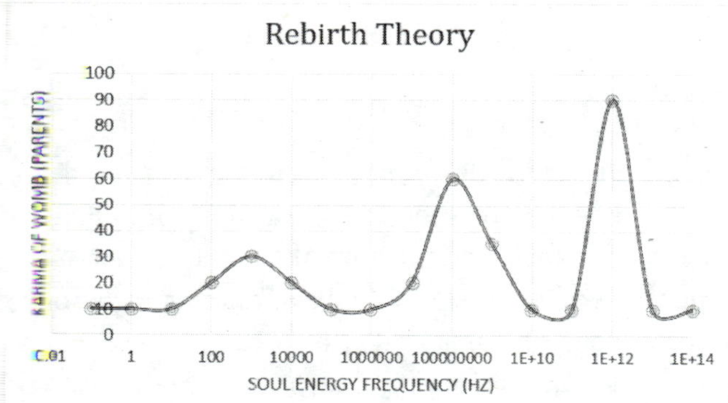

Let us take the example of *Rajssic* (राजसिक) man's soul. After death, the soul is in the air and tries to find the right womb, a materialistic body. It is just like radio waves. When the waves (songs) are transmitted from the station, the waves are in the air and it is everywhere. If one tunes the radio, then the songs come on the radio. Similarly, when the *Rajssic* soul finds a right womb (fertilised), it attaches with the *Rajssic* womb, and life starts. The *Rajssic* soul attaches only to the *Rajssic* womb because of the resonance in the energy. The *Rajssic* soul cannot attach with the womb of *Tamssic* (तामसिक) or the *Sattvic* (सात्विक) womb. This is the basic principle in physics, and based on this principle, we believe the *Karmic* theory plays an important role for the rebirth. As already mentioned soul (सूक्षम-शरीर) consists of *Atama* and spirit. The *Karmas* influence is on the spirit only, not on the *Atama* (self), which provides the consciousness to the materialistic body (mind).

Why is the आत्मा (self) changeless?

23. Weapons cannot cut it, nor can the fire burn it. Water cannot wet it, nor can the air dry it.

> "इस आत्मा को शस्त्र नही काटते, इसे अग्नि नही जलाती, इसे पानी नही गीला करता और न पवन (हवा) ही सुखाता है I"

The changeless, Immutable *Atama* (self) is described by Lord Krishna in terms of a mutable and ever-changing world, which is very familiar to Arjuna and all people like us. In the world of change, objects come to their end (annihilation) either through the instruments of death, are consumed by fire, destroyed by water, or dried up by air. These are the various cosmic means and methods by which the objects of the world come to their destruction. All these means are declared as not capable (impotent) of bringing about the destruction of the self (*Atama*).

What reason, why, and how can we recognise *Atama* (self) to be Eternal?

24. The *Atama* is unsplitable, incombustible, and cannot be wetted and dried. It is undoubtedly permanent, all-pervading, immovable, constant and everlasting.

"यह आत्मा काटा नही जा सकता, यह जलाया नही जा सकता, यह भिगोया नही जा सकता और ना सुखाया ही जा सकता है I यह नित्य, सबमें भिदा हुआ, स्थिर, अचल और सनातन है I"

25. The self *(Atama)* is said to be un-manifested, unthinkable and unchanging. Therefore, knowing it as such, it is not proper for you to grieve over it.

"यह आत्मा अव्यक्त, अचिंत्य, और अविनाशी कहा जाता है I अन्त इसे एवविध जानकर तुम्हे शोक करना उचित नही है I"

It is amply clear that if a thing cannot be finished or annihilated by any known methods of destruction of nature, or by those invented and perfected by man, then that given object must be everlasting. All-pervading is a short term of inconceivable depth of significance. All-pervading is that which pervades everywhere. All-pervading (like water, air, fire, space) has no shape, since that which has a shape is conditioned all along its outline by something other than itself. A truth that is thus Eternal (नित्य), Homogeneous, and All-pervading (सर्वगत), must necessarily be stable (स्थिर), because no change can ever take place in it. That which is thus stable must be 'firm' (अचल), for it cannot shake or move, since movement implies the transfer of a thing from one set of time and place to another set of time and place, where it was not. Since the *Atama* (self) is All-pervading, there is no spot in space, or period in time, where it is not already, and therefore, just as I cannot myself, the self cannot move anywhere. A motionless thing is indeed 'Firm' (अचल). The *Atama* is not new (नया), but it is an ancient concept, and therefore, we as students of *Brahma-Vidya* need not hesitate to accept it, because we necessarily would, if the theory were a modern ideology which was yet to be verified by observed scientific data. The *Atama* is unconditioned by time and place, perfection gained, whether it is in India or at the north pole, in the present generation, or the chaste periods of Vedic culture, in all places and at all times, by all seers, in all religions of the world, the *Atama* (self)-experience at the time of God-realisation, can only be the same.

This Eternal, All-pervading *Atama* is certainly un-manifest, unthinkable, and unchangeable, and therefore, having known this truth in its essential nature, Krishna argues that it is neither possible to kill nor to get really killed in the context of the war in the *Mahabharata*. However, the embodied body can be killed, and to kill or not to kill depends upon the *Dharma* (consciousness). Each of these terms is quite expressive of a certain logical truth.

Un-manifest – A thing is called manifest when we can perceive it through one or other sense organs. That which is beyond all the five sense-organs is called Unmanifest. I cannot see, smell, hear, taste or touch a full-grown mango tree in a mango seed, and yet I know that the seed is the cause for the tree. Under the circumstances, the tree is said to be in 'un-manifest' condition within the seed. Similarly, when they say that truth is un-manifest, they only mean that it cannot be perceived through any of our sense organs.

Unthinkable – After denying the sense-organs any play in the field of truth, we are told that the human mind also cannot think, nor can human intellect ruminate (think) over, and comprehend the infinite. The *Atama* being the very life that energies the mind and the intellect and not the vice-versa, which by themselves are inert and insertient; it becomes obvious that the mind and the intellect cannot make the *Atama* (self) an object of their comprehension. A telescope-gazer cannot see himself with his telescope; he cannot be at once to see and the seen. Thus, here the Lord's word 'Unthinkable' is to be understood as meaning 'Incomprehensible' by the mind and the intellect of the seeker.

Unchangeable – This term indicates that the *Atama* is without parts because things that have parts in themselves are things which have 'Form' and those that have form must necessarily come under the category of the FINITE, and exhibit in themselves various modifications and changes.

Krishna thus advises Arjuna to end his grief. He who understands the Eternal nature of *Atama* (self) can have neither the occasion to perceive himself as the slayer, nor recognise others as a slain.

26. Even if you believe it to be constantly born and dying, even then, O mighty armed (Arjuna), you should not grieve over it.

"पर यदि तू आत्मा को नित्य जन्म लेनेवाला और नित्य मरनेवाला ही मानता है, तो भी हे महाबाहु, तुझे इस सम्बन्ध में शोक करना उचित नही I"

27. Death is certain for one who is born, and birth is certain who dies. Therefore, you should not grieve over the inevitable.

"कारन यह है कि जिसका जन्म होता है, उसकी म्रत्यु भी निश्चित है और जिस की म्रत्यु होती है, उसका जन्म भी निश्चित है I अंत: ऐसी अपरिहार्य बातो के लिए शोक करना तुझे उचित नही I"

Lord Krishna explains to Arjuna from a materialistic or scientific view, direct perception alone is an authority for belief. With this standard for their knowledge, when they try to measure life, they have to accept it as a constant flux of infinite lives and infinite deaths. Things are born, and they have to die away. This whirl of birth and death is constant. And constant change is life to them. Krishana argues if life is but a constant repletion of birth and death, then also the hero (महाबाहु) that you are, you do not deserve to grieve on the occasion.

That which is born must die, and after death things are born again. Here, Krishna continues to view the whole situation from a materialist's angle. The materialists think that life is a constant flood of appearances of forms arising from nowhere and disappearing into nowhere. Scientifically also it is also not possible, because the energy cannot come from nothing. The form of energy changes from potential to kinetic or from heat to electric or from nuclear to electric or vice versa. Theists believe that embodiments are taken up by the individual-ego in order that it may eke out its experiences and learn to grow in its understanding of life and ultimately realise the truth behind it all. Thus, this is a common meeting point of both theists and atheists, that both of them believe life to be a continuous chain of birth and death.

28. O Bharata (Arjuna), all beings are unmanifested before birth, and they will be unmanifested after death. They only manifest in the intervening period. Then, where is room for grief?

"हे भरतवंशी अर्जुन, विश्व के समस्त चर और अचर पदार्थ प्रारंभ में अव्यक्त होते है, केवल बिच में व्यक्त दीखते है और अन्त में फिर से अव्यक्त हो जाते है I ऐसी स्थिती में भला दुःख करने की कौनसी बात है I"

Now the Lord Krishna explains the problem as viewed through the goggles of a common man or materialistic people of the world and valued by their intellect judgements, the manifest-world of today (let us say the mango seed) was un-manifested (Mango seed) before its creation; and now for time being it is available for cognition (sensation) as fully manifested (full tree). But after a few years it fades away (dies) into the unmanifested again (mango seed). It amounts to saying that the present came from the unknown and shall return to the unknown. Krishna says to Arjuna that even if viewed thus, why should one moan? For the spokes of the wheel that turn eternally must come down only to rise up again.

29. Some look at it (*Atama*) as a wonder, some speak of it as a wonder, and some hear of it as a wonder; but even after this hearing, no one really knows it.

"कोई इस आत्मा को आश्चर्य के समान देखता है, कोई दूसरा इसका आश्चर्य के समान कथन करता है और कोई इसे आश्चर्य के समान सुनता है तथा कोई तो सुनकर भी नही जान पाता I"

The existence of the subtler *Atama* (self) beyond the body, the mind, and the intellect is an idea that cannot even be conceived by the ego-centric people. Some see it as a wonder and some speak as magical, and some hear with surprise. Even after hearing, speaking and thinking no one really knows about the self. However, the rarest of the rare can see or speak or think about the *Atama* (self). Therefore, *Atama*'s presence in the body is rarely known or felt.

If one talks about self or *Atama* in scientific terms, it is nothing but consciousness. Different views and different theories are given regarding consciousness, but nobody knows about it. Although everybody knows it and feels it but its (consciousness) presence is still a mystery in the scientific world, like the self or *Atama* in spirituality.

Who knows the *Atama* (self)?

30. O Bharata (Arjuna), the dweller in the body (*Atama*) is indestructible in all beings. Therefore, it is not logical that you should grieve about them.

“हे भरत, शरीर के भीतर रहनेवाला उसका स्वामी यह आत्मा सभी शरिरो में सदेव अवध्य रूप से विध्यमान है, अतएव तुझे किसी प्राणी के लिए शोक करना उचित नही I”

The subtle reality in each body that is the indwelling soul, along with the spirit, in every creature is Eternal and indestructible. All that is destroyed is only the container, the finite matter envelopment. Therefore, Arjuna has been advised that he should not grieve upon facing his enemies and in the great battle, even in killing them, if need be. To bring out this idea, the entire earlier section has been used by Krishna, wherein he argued so well to establish the Eternal nature of the soul and the finite nature of the bodies.

What Lord Krishna is trying to tell Arjuna is that the self (*Atama*) is formless or sizeless, therefore, cannot be finished. Air, water, ether, fire etc, are the creations of the Almighty and cannot be destroyed. Similarly, *Atama* (self) is a small part of the Almighty and hence cannot be destroyed. Knowledge and happiness are the quality of self (*Atama*) and not the materialistic body. The body functions is to do *Karmas (Gunas*), and *Atama* (self) is the enjoyer of it. The materialistic body is a part of the materialistic world and hence perishable, whereas *Atama* (self) is a part of the Almighty and hence imperishable.

What is *Dharma* (धर्म)

31. Further, considering your own *Dharma* (duty), you should not falter, because for a Kshatriya, there is nothing more meritorious than a righteous war.

> "और स्वधर्मे को देखते हुए भी तुम (इस प्रकार) डावाडोल होने योग्य नही हो, क्योकि शत्रिय के लिए धर्मयुद्ध से बड़कर कल्याणकर और कुछ नही है I"

32. O' Partha, this war, which is an open door to heaven, falls (unsolicited) to the lot of fortunate *Kshetriya.*

> "हे पार्थ, अपने आप प्राप्त खुले स्वर्गद्वार की तरह इस प्रकार के धर्म-युद्ध को भाग्यवान शत्रिय लोग ही प्राप्त करते है I"

In the Indian context "*Dharma*" is used in many ways; therefore, it creates some confusion. It is used for religious purposes like Hindu, Christian or Islamic *Dharma*, or it is being used even for sub-casts like Kshatriya, Vaishas or Brahman *Dharma*. In Bhagwat-*Geeta* (ch.4-13) the *Swadharma* (स्वधर्म) was defined on the basis of *Gunas and Karmas* and not on the basis of birth. Even for a profession for a longer duration, and if he becomes an expert in that field, like teaching or medical work, then it becomes his *Dharma*. In other words, that particular profession is in his *Gunas* and called his *Dharma*. *Dharma* is also defined as duty also, for example, parents have the duty towards their children to give a good education and take the proper care which means it is the parents' *Dharma* towards their children.

In verse 31, the *Swadharma* (स्वधर्म) is very important, which is applicable in today's era also. The equivalent word for *Swadharma* in English is THE PATH OF LEAST RESISTANCE. There are mainly two layers of *Swadharma*, one is from inside and another is from outside. The inside layer defines your mental get-up or aptitude, which also comes from past life. The outside layer depends upon your family background (or cast). If a boy wants to become a soldier and his family background is also in defence, then it is easy for him to go into defence, or we call it is his *Swadharma*. A boy from a doctor's family wants to become a businessman, then it is not his *Swadharma* for him. If we think of Arjuna, Bhima or Duryodhana, their family background was of a royal family, and their aptitude (interest) was also in fighting, so it is their *Swadharma*. However, Yudhishtra's aptitude was in knowledge (spirituality), but he was forced into war; therefore, it was not his *Swadharma* in the *Mahabharta*.

Arjuna's personal call-of-character (स्वधर्म) is that of a leader of his generation (क्षेत्रिय) and as such, when his generation is called upon to answer a challenge of an organised un-*Aryan* force (अधर्म), it is his duty not to waver but to fight and defend his sacred national culture. To the leaders of the people, there can be nothing nobler than to get a glorious chance to fight for a righteous cause. Here, Arjuna has been called upon to fight a righteous war wherein his enemies are true aggressors. Therefore, it is said that such a chance comes indeed, only for a lucky few. That a king must fight on such an occasion is vividly brought out in the *Mahabharta*.

As used here, *Kshatriya* is not the name of the caste. It merely indicates a certain quality of mental *Vasanas* in the individual. Those who have ever-bubbling enthusiasm to defend a weak and the poor, besides their own national culture, from all threats of aggression are called *Kshatriyas*. The Hindu nation is forced to wage a war on the principles of righteousness (Upapannam), leaders of India are ordered to fight in defence of their culture and to consider themselves fortunate to get a chance to serve the country. Such battlefields are wide-open gates to Heaven for the defending heroes who fight diligently on the side of *Dharma*.

It is indeed a fact that it is your duty, and now, in case you renounce it and run away from the battlefield, then:

33. But if you do not engage in this righteous war, you will be incurring a sin as a result of abandoning your *Dharma* and reputation.

"और यदि तू यह धर्मयुद्ध संग्राम नही करेगा, तो अपना धर्म और यश दोनों खोकर पाप का भागी बनेगा I"

In case you refuse to engage yourself in the glorious war, then not only will you be renouncing your own personal call-of-character (स्वधर्म) and honour, in not having fulfilled your noble duty, but will also incur a positive sin. Not to face this army of un-*Aryan* forces is as much sinful as to murder those who do not deserve such treatment.

Not to make use of the evolutionary chances provided by life is to reject and refuse the chances provided for a *Vasana*-catharsis (relief). By not exhausting the old bad-*Vasana*, one will be living under high *Vasanas*-pressure when the existing tendencies are crowded out by the influx of new tendencies. Not fighting the war, Arjuna may run away from the field, but he will certainly come to regret his lost chances, since his mind is so composed that he can find complete relief and solace only by living the intensely dangerous life of the battlefield. A boy with a tendency towards art cannot be successfully trained to become a businessman or an economist, since these are contrary to his nature (*Gunas*). If an over-anxious parent, in the name of love, projects upon a growing child his intentions and plans, we invariably find that the young boy will have a crushed personality.

34. People, too, will recount your everlasting dishonour, and to the one who has been honoured, dishonour is more than death.

> "यही नही, बल्कि सब लोग तेरी अक्षय अपकीर्ति का गान करते रहेगे, और ऐसा अपयश तो सन्मानित पुरुष के लिए मृत्यु से भी बड़कर है I"

35. The great battalion commanders will think that you have withdrawn from the battle through fear, and you will be looked down upon by those who had thought too much of you and your heroism in the past.

> "वे महारथी लोग, जिनके लिए तू बड़ा माननीय है, सोचेगे कि तू भय के कारन युद्ध से विरत हो गया है और इस प्रकार उनके पास तू अब बड़ा तुच्छ हो जायेगा I"

36. And many unspeakable words will your enemies speak, cavilling about your powers. What can be more painful than this?

> “तेरे वैरी लोग तेरी सामर्थ्य की निंदा करते हुए ऐसी बहुत-सी बाते कहगे, जो न कहनी चाहिए I इससे बड़कर दुःख की बात क्या होगी?”

To a famous hero, dishonour is worse than death. This is another argument that Krishna brings forth to persuade his friend to give up his hesitation in fighting the Great War. The general import is that if Arjuna were to abandon the fight, he could do so only because of his cowardice, since the cause of the war is righteous. Certainly, there is an undercurrent of sympathy in Krishna’s words as he realises that, however great a hero Arjuna might be, even he could be weakened by wrong emotionalism.

Continuing the common man’s point of view arguments, Krishna says here that not only will the world blame him and history recounts his infamy, but immediately the great warriors and battalion commanders (महारथी) in the enemy lines will also start ridiculing him. They will laugh at him and say that the great archer Arjuna ran away from the battlefront because of sheer cowardice. They will interpret his conscientious objections against the fratricidal war as an act of cowardice by a hero during a weak moment in his life. No soldier can stand such dishonour, especially when it comes from one’s own equals among the enemy lines.

Finding that Arjuna is conspicuously reacting well to these arguments, Krishna drives home to him the folly of running away from the battlefield. It will be intolerable when his enemies scandalise his glorious name and his chivalry in foul language, too indecent even for words. Not only will history record for all times his cowardly retreat, but even while he lives, he will be pointed out and laughed at as a 'hero' who ran away from the battlefront.

37. Either you will attain heaven on death or enjoy the sovereignty of this land as a result of your victory. Therefore, O Kaunteya (Arjuna), stand up determined to fight.

"या तो युद्ध में मरकर स्वर्ग को प्राप्त करेगा अथवा जीतकर प्रथ्वी का भोग करेगाI अतएव हे अर्जुन, युद्ध करने का द्रडसंकल्प ले उठ खड़ा हो I"

In case he has to give his life on the warfront while fighting for such a noble cause, he shall certainly enter the 'heaven of heroes' (वीर-स्वर्ग) to stay and to enjoy there for aeons (forever). In case he wins, he shall certainly come to rule over the kingdom and enjoy the world, and thereafter he shall go to Heaven to enjoy there the status of mighty hero who fought championing the cause of *Dharma*. Either way, he will gain because he was on the side of the good, with the war aims of the *Pandavas* being stoutly righteous. Therefore, meaning, for all the reasons so far enumerated, "Arise, resolve to fight." Earlier on, Arjuna, after expressing his feelings of grief and despair, had sat down inert and motionless upon throwing down his weapons, Krishna asks his friend to come out of this moodiness and dejection, and be determined to fight the noble war.

The call to war is justified because of the particular situation in the *Mahabharta,* wherein the *Geeta* was given out. Generalising the call of Krishna, we may say that it is a divine call to a man to discard his melancholy (sadness) dejection in the face of life's challenges and to come forward to play as best as he can 'the game of life' with a firm determination to strive and to win. In this line, we have the universality of the *Geeta* explicitly brought out for those who understand and find its vast application to the community of man.

Krishna advises Arjuna on the inner attitude, why he should fight the battle.

38. Considering alike, pleasure and pain, gain and loss, victory and defeat, engage yourself in battle. Fighting this way, you will not incur sin.

“सुख और दुःख, लाभ और हानि, जय और पराजय को समान समझते हुए युद्ध में प्रव्रत हो जा I इसमें तुझे पाप छु न सकेगा I”

In this stanza, Krishna tries to explain how he should conduct himself in this undertaking. He says that he should fight the war with perfect detachment from all anxieties which generally come to an individual, when he identifies himself with the non-self (अनात्मा or desire prompted), meaning that at the level of his intellect with the concept of pain and pleasure, at the level of his mind with the fears of gain and loss, and at his body-level with the restlessness of conquest and defeat, in that case, he would not incur any sin.

Here, Lord says to Arjuna that once you know the war is for the right cause, then you fight with your enemies with perfect detachment from the results of the war. Acting this way, even if you kill many people, you will not have any sin. It is clear that in any given situation, one can attain perfection in life.

Generally, our actions happen due to desire or due to duty (*Dharma*). If *Karmas* are due to desire, then sin may happen, and if it is due to *Dharma* (duty) bound actions, sin will never touch such actions. Arjuna is doing war for the *Dharma* and not for enjoying the kingdom after winning the war; therefore, whatever sin happens by killing soldiers in the war, will never touch him, which is given in Sankhya philosophy by Kapila.

Karma-Yoga, without attachments

Now, Krishna explains the *Karma*-YOGA from the Vedantic philosophy, given by Maharshi Patanjali.

39. O Partha, this attitude of mind is imparted to you following Sankhya-Yoga, and now hear this according to *karma*-Yoga. Armed with knowledge, you will cast away the bonds of *Karmas*.

"हे पार्थ, तुझे सांख्य-सम्बधी बुद्धि बतलाई गई, पर अब तू योग-सम्बधी सुन, जिस बुद्धि से युक्त होकर तू कर्मबन्धन को काट लेगा I"

In the above shloka, Lord Krishna told Arjuna how to conduct his *Karmas* in the war based on 'Sankhya-philosophy, meaning, the logic of reasoning by which the true nature of reality is comprehended. Now in this verse he advises him based on Maharshi Patanjali's Yoga and termed as *Karma*-Yoga. The Lord has taken the meaning only from both philosophies, but not from actual philosophy for the *Karma*-Yoga.

Lord tells Arjuna the knowledge of self (Atamagyan/आत्मज्ञान) based on *Karmyoga*. To have the knowledge of the self, the intelligence (बुद्धि) should be pure, which is done by listening, thinking and repetition. Listening and thinking are possible when your mind is at peace (not agitated), and that is possible when you have the *Sattvic Gunas* in the personality. *Sattvic Gunas* is obtained by doing *Sattvic Karmas*, which is luminous because of the purity of thoughts, where attachment, desires, and anger are at their minimum level. It has neither the dullness of *Rajas* nor dark impurities of *Tamas*. Under the *Sattvic* influence, the mind is steady, reflecting ever faithfully the consciousness from the self. This is not a quick process, and one has to practice these habits in actual life, then only one is ready to know the knowledge of self (*Atama*). Even for the *Gyan*-yogi (संन्यासी), he also has to go through this type of *Karma*-yoga. Once the *Karma*-yogi acquires the knowledge of self (Atamayogi/आत्मयोगी) then his *Karmas* become unbinding on him. According to Adi Shankaracharya, *Sannyasa* is the final goal, and *Karma*-yoga is the way for *Gyan*-Yoga (*Sannyasi*), however, according to

B.G.Tilak, even after acquiring the *Sannyasi*, one has to do the *Karmas* for the society and common people.

40. In *Karma* - Yoga, there is no loss of effort nor any sin accrues as a result of some lapse while doing the *Kasmas*. A little practice of *Karma*-Yoga protects you from the great danger of the life and death cycle.

"इस निष्काम कर्मयोग में आरम्भ किए का नाश नही है और कर्म का उलटा परिणाम भी नही होता I इस कर्मयोगरूप धर्म का थोडा सा अनुष्ठान भी बहुत बड़े भय से रक्शा कर देता है I"

There is a danger in the field of activities of unfinished ritualistic acts by which we are cheated of all our expected results. Krishna here established his own philosophy that his technique of action, i.e. *Karma*-Yoga, guarantees safety from this main danger, and that danger is unequanimity of intellect.

Unfinished ritualistic acts will yield no fruits, just as ploughing and sowing are not fulfilled, if the sequence of actions as ploughing, watering, weeding, guarding, harvesting etc., are not kept exactly in that order. Similarly, some ritualistic acts, when not performed faithfully following all strict injunctions, the chances are that the same meritorious acts might result in sins accrued through the non-performance, or imperfect performance of enjoined acts. In the material world also, we can find corresponding instances wherein a medicine misused may bring about calamities for the patient. But *Karma*-Yoga guarantees safety from such dangers.

41. O Kurunandana (Arjuna), the intellect of a determinate mind is only one, whereas the reasoning (intellect) of an irresolute mind is infinite and many-branched.

“हे अर्जुन, इस निष्कर्म में सुनिश्चित ज्ञान एक ही होता है I पर जो अस्थिर मनवाले है, उनकी बुद्धि अनेक शाका-प्रशाखाओ में विभक्त तथा अनन्त प्रकार की है I”

In *Karma*-Yoga, which the Lord is now explaining, even the highest achievement of self-realisation is possible, because here, the main work, done with resolute determination, with a single-pointed mind. If an individual can entertain any single resolute determination, and an action consistently directed towards its success, achievements must certainly result. But invariably, man, when victimised by his ego, entertains hundreds of desires, resulting in multiple actions that are often mutually contradictory, and therefore, he comes to play upon these fields with an impoverished and exhausted mental strength. This is psychologically what we call “self-cancellation of thought”, where this activity comes to plague the mental zone, it exhausts all the potentiality of man and loots away all his chances of success.

If you want to become successful in *Karma*-Yoga, the only thing one has to do is focus on intelligence (determination), and it can be a spiritual or materialistic goal. In the spiritual goal, the most important thing is to first develop the *Sattvic Gunas* and try to have a minimum ego, lust, anger and attachments. For the materialistic world, first decide the goal intellectually and see its positive and negative aspects. Once you are convinced the goal is perfect, then work hard, try again and again, that is called single-pointed intellect (व्यवसायात्मक-बुद्धि). The general tendency of the mind is for the desires, lust, ego, etc., which disturb the intellect. Do not allow the mind to rule the intellect but rule the mind by using the conscious intellect (विवेक-बुद्धि), so that the mind does not wander and your intellect is focused on the goal. However, your intellect should not be on the fruits of action, and this is nothing but *Karma*-Yoga only. Similarly, Krishna tells Arjuna that the war's positive and negative aspects have been considered thoroughly, and it is for the right cause; therefore, your goal should be to fight in this war without expecting the results of the war.

If your intellect is not focused and your intellect is many-branched, then what its effects are explained in the following three verses.

42. Flowery speech is uttered by the unwise, taking pleasure in the eulogising words of the Vedas, O Partha, saying, "there is nothing else."

"हे पार्थ, जो अविवेकी जन है, वे केवल वेदोके काम्य कर्मो की प्रशंसा में रत रहते है I इस मत के पोषक है कि स्वर्ग प्रदान करनेवाले कर्मो के अतिरिक्त जीवन में और कुछ भी कर्तव्य नही है I"

The one, who has multiple desires talks about the Vedas in flowery words and tries to have *Karma* fruits only. They also say that by doing only *Karmas* one can attain heaven. Lord Krishna says such people are fools and do not use their inner consciousness for any problem.

43. Full of desires, having heaven as their goal, they utter flowery words, which promise new birth as the reward for their actions, and prescribe various specific actions for the attainment of pleasure and Lordship.

'वे कामना से भरे हुए तथा स्वर्ग-लाभ में ही परम पुरुषार्थ माननेवाले लोग सदैव ऐसी वाणी बोलते रहते है, जो सुनने में बड़ी आकर्षक और लुभावनी लगती है तथा जो अनेक प्रकार की ऐसी क्रियाओ का ही वर्णन करते रहते है, जिनका उदेश्य जन्म-रूप फल देना तथा सुख-भोग और आश्वर्य प्रदान करना होता है I"

44. For those who cling to joy and Lordship, whose minds are drawn away by such teaching, are neither determinate nor resolute; they are not fit for steady meditation and *Samandhi.*

"उस वाणी से जिनका चित हर लिया जाता है, ऐसे भोग और आश्चर्य में आसक्त लोगों का कार्य-अकार्य का निश्चय करनेवाली बुद्धि, चित में एकाग्र नही हो पाती, अर्थात ऐसे लोगों को व्यवसयात्मक-बुद्धि नही प्राप्त होती I"

Maharshi Vyasa was one of the first daring revolutionaries in Hinduism who ever came up to win back the Hindu culture from the decadence it had fallen into, in his time. The Bible of the revolution that he created was the *Geeta*. His vigorous criticism is reflected in the words of Krishna, he characterises "the ritualistic portion of the Vedas as the flowering words of the unwise". We have to live mentally in the orthodox atmosphere of that age to appreciate the daringness with which Vyasa then had to put up this criticism so strongly.

The ritualistic sections (Priests, Pujaris, Pandiths etc) of the Vedas address those who are deeply attached to pleasures and power, whose discriminative power, the capacity to distinguish the Real from Unreal, is stolen away from the people, because they are concerned about the results of their own *Karmas.* The ritualists were involved in the ritualism as such and not concerned with the Higher, to reach which these (rituals) are but the means. These rituals, *Karmas,* which promised the performer a post-mortem heavenly existence with supra-sensuous carnal pleasures, are to be undertaken and laboriously pursued. In all these activities, man's inner personality has no time or chance to get integrated and evolve. Therefore, from the spiritual standpoint, Vyasa felt that their methods of impotent (useless) religion. The ritualist gets involved in the means, without aspiring for the Real god. The persons who are tossed about by their desires shall never get any experience of tranquillity in their inner life.

Krishna is here laughing at those who mistake the means for the end. The ritualistic portion is the means, and the Vedantic portion dealing with realisation through meditation is the end. The *Karma-kanda* prepares the mind to single-pointedness, when it is pursued without specific desires (निष्कर्म). Such a prepared mind alone is fit for steady contemplation over the Upanishadic declarations.

The Lord now speaks about the result accruing to those Lustful persons who are lacking in discrimination.

45. O Arjuna, the Vedas enumerate the three *Gunas* (qualities). Rise above these qualities, be free from the pairs of opposites, steadfast in the eternal, detached from the worldly possessions and their acquisition, and become devoted to *Atama* (established in self).

"हे अर्जुन, वेद सत्व, रज, और तम इन तीनो गुणो को अपना विषय बनाते है अर्थात इन तीनो गुणों से उत्पन संसार ही वेदों का प्रकाशीत है, तू तो इन तीनों गुणों से ऊपर उठ जा I सुख-दुःख दव्न्दो से अतीत हो सर्वदा सत्व अर्थात नित्य वस्तु में स्थित रह I योग और शेम की चिंता का त्याग कर, आत्मा में प्रतिष्टित हो I"

According to the Vedic teaching, the world is made up of three *Gunas* (qualities). The *Sattva* (pureness), *Rajas* (passion) and the *Tamas* (laziness), all these qualities are in the bosom of every human being in different proportions. There is a way to go to the *Sattva* by suppressing the *Rajas Gunas*. *Tamas Gunas* can be suppressed by raising to the *Rajas Gunas*. Once you develop the *Sattva Gunas,* try to spend your life in *Sattva*, which is the highest state in the Vedas, where one can have peace in the mind. Generally, we get confused between happiness and peacefulness. We think that if we are happy, then peacefulness will come, which is a wrong concept. Happiness is the state of the materialistic body and the sense organs. But peacefulness is a state of mind. Happiness disturbs your intellect, and so the sorrow. Therefore, Krishna advises Arjuna to try to develop the first *Sattva* quality. But this is not the highest state for the *Gyanni* or *Sannyasi* (ज्ञानी/सन्यासी/wisdom). One has to remain always in contact with self (*Atama* or consciousness) for a *Sanny*asi where he (Arjuna) is lacking these qualities.

The three inseparable *Gunas* always remain in the inner constitution of every living creature, in varying proportions. Tea is made up of hot water, tea leaves, sugar and milk. From a cup of tea, if you are asked to remove these three components, it amounts to saying 'empty the cup'. Now the empty cup is ready to be filled by some other thing. The nearest thing to mind and intellect cup is the self. Therefore, once all three *Gunas* are dropped, which means outer-*Atama* (spirit) is like inner-*Atama* (self). The mind will have direct contact with *Atama* (inner-consciousness). In the language of Upnishadas (उपनिषद), man has been advised to transcend the mind and the intellect, and they promise that the individual shall thereby rediscover himself, *Atama* (self), which is the part of God.

The second line in the stanza gives us a very practical and direct method of transporting ourselves from the realm of imperfection to the boundless regions of Bliss and Beatitude. Earlier, Krishna had indicated how Arjuna should enter the field and wage a war. The same mental equanimity is being advised here in a different language. Pairs-of-opposite are the experiences in our life, such as joy and sorrow, health and disease, success and failure, heat and cold, etc. Each of them can be experienced and known only regarding and as a contrast to its opposite. Therefore, the term 'pairs-of-opposite' (द्वन्द्व) envisages in its comprehensive meaning all the experiences of man in his life. Krishna advises Arjuna to be free from all the 'opposites'.

Yog (meaning to acquire) and *Kshema* (means preserving the acquired things) in their meanings include all activities of every human being in the universe. These are the two urges which goad everyone in all of one's activities. Thus, the two terms *Yog and Kshema* encompass all our egocentric activities motivated by our selfish desires to acquire and compelled by the equally selfish wishes to hoard and preserve what has been acquired. To renounce these two temperaments is to get away immediately from the two main fields that yield the poisonous harvest of extreme restlessness and sorrow of life.

It is very easy for a spiritual master to advise an aspirant to be "free from the pair-of-opposite", remain ever pure and free from natural appetites for acquisition, and from the usual greed and preservation. But the philosophy can be practical only when the seeker is advised on how he can do so. This 'how' of it all has been indicated by the last word in the stanza: (आत्मवान), meaning "be established in the self." The persecutions of the pairs-of-opposites, the instinct to be impure, the desire to possess, and the anxiety to preserve, all of these belong to the ego-centre, which is born when the self identifies with the body, the mind and the intellect, and consequent ego suffers the pangs of anxieties, pains and sorrows.

When established in the self, the individual ego that becomes pure and free from all anxieties finds itself beyond the experience of the world. Necessarily, he will be trans-*Gunas.* One who is beyond *Gunas,* then there is no use for the Vedas textbooks. He is the master thereafter who shall give the divine sanction for these Vedic declarations.

Then, up to what extent the Vedas are useful is given in the following shloka:

46. An enlightened *Brahman* has as much use for all the Vedas as a person has a small reservoir of water when he acquires a vast land of flooded water.

“सब ओर धरती के जलमग्न होने पर कुए, पोखरे, तलाब आदि छोटे-छोटे जलाश्यो का जितना प्रयोजन रह जाता है, उतना ही प्रयोजन ब्रह्म को जाननेवाले के लिए सारे वेदों का रह जाता है I”

This shloka has been interpreted in different ways by different spiritualists. Some write that Krishna has criticised the Vedas, and some say it is a preliminary step for understanding spirituality. Basically, Vedic knowledge deals with the triple quality temperaments *(Gunas)* for a happy life. Once you have happiness, then only you can get spiritual knowledge (अध्यात्म). To attend the *Sattvic* (pureness), one has to go through the Vedas only. But after that, one can have the knowledge of self *(Atma)*. If the area is surrounded by a flood of water, then the importance of Vedas is just like wells, ponds, etc., for a *Gyani* or *Sannyasi*. However, for the common people, Vedas are important and may not be useful for the *Sannyasi.* It is just like a student of maths, upon having successfully passed a postgraduate course, need not read the arithmetic tables, since his greater knowledge comprehends this elementary study.

Another interpretation of this shloka is that when water is flooded everywhere, still there is importance of wells and ponds for drinking because we cannot drink water from flooded ones. Similarly, for a man-of-wisdom (संन्यासी), he still needs the knowledge of Vedas for living in the materialistic world or for day-to-day activities. Therefore, *Geeta* does not criticise the Vedas but supports for spiritual knowledge of the aspirants.

In the following verse, Krishna tells Arjuna that to become a *Sannyasi* (a man of wisdom) you can attain by doing *Karmas* and not by leaving them.

47. Your right extends only to the performance of action. Fruits of action should not be your object. Furthermore, do not be attached to inaction.

"तेरा अधिकार कर्म करने मे ही है, उनके फलों में कभी भी नही I तु कर्मफल प्राप्ति का कारण मत बन और न तेरी प्रव्रति कर्म करने में है I"

The fundamental truth is never to strive with a mind dissipated with anxieties and fear about the fruits. In fact, the reward of the action, when we understand it properly, is not anything different from the action itself. An action done in the PRESENT, which is conditioned (planned) by the FUTURE-time, appears as the fruit of the action. An action performed in the present, when defined in terms of a future moment, is its reaction. Therefore, to worry over and get ourselves preoccupied with the anxieties for the rewards of actions is to escape from the dynamic PRESENT moment and live in a FUTURE moment that is not yet born. In short, Lord's advice here is a call to man not to waste his present moments in fruitless dreams and fears, but to bring out his best, in all of the best form within him, to PRESENT moment and vitally live every moment. The promise is that the future will take care of itself. If it is a failure, then leave it to the Divine supreme and try to learn the reasons for failure.

The results of our actions are not in our control. It is a common experience that sometimes our best- laid plans are thwarted by unknown forces beyond our control. It is easy to satisfy one's ego by explaining away the future on one pretext or the other without accepting the unseen hand of nature. But often times the natural phenomena and the inexplicable are to be brushed aside. This is true in all walks of life and is the main cause of our unhappiness and frustration.

An inevitable question arises that if we have no control over the outcome of our actions, then why to bother about them at all? Instead of struggling in this world for personal and societal advancement, the easier course would be to lead the life of a mendicant and avoid the pains and going of day-to-day struggles. This, however, is not sound logic. The renunciation of action to escape the pain and misery does not take into account the consequences that will follow in adopting this course. Life minus action is equal to death.

With sense organs (eyes, ears, tongue, nose and skin) in place and controlled by the mind. It is impossible to renounce action. Besides these, human beings are also endowed with organs of action. The qualities of these are pre-determined. They function in spite of our efforts to the contrary. So, how is the renunciation of action possible? Furthermore, action is necessary to support life. Whether you spend life as a lazy, a hard-working labourer, or an intellectual, a professional, a businessman, an ascetic, or whatever vocation might be, you need food to maintain the body and other necessities for your existence. Who is going to supply food and these necessities of life? Action, therefore, becomes essential. Having realised that action is necessary to sustain life. Furthermore, since action is unavoidable because of the inherent qualities of sense organs and the mind, the concept of renouncing action becomes sheer hypocrisy. Action is imperative for living beings.

The basic tenet of *Karma*-Yoga is that one must perform righteous action without desire for any reward. Stealing, murder, and the like are also actions, but they are righteous and decidedly forbidden and must be avoided at all costs. There is no sin attached to the performance of one's duty (*Dharma)*. This form of Yoga is easy to practice as compared to other forms of Yoga concepts. A *Karma*-Yogi is endowed with balanced reasoning and is freed from the pairs of opposites, such as pleasure and pain, gain and loss, sorrow and happiness and reaches a state where there is nothing but happiness.

Three views of doing Karmas:

Some men think I will do *Karma* for the fruits of action, and some think if I don't get fruits, I will not do the *Karmas.* The first type of attitude is called *Rajssic* (Passivity) and the second type is called *Tamssic* (Laziness). The third type, which is mentioned in the shloka, is that he does *Karmas (Sattva)* but without expecting the fruits of action. Then one can question, if he does not expect fruits, then he will not get any motivation for doing *Karmas.* Krishna tells Arjuna that for a man of wisdom, his motivation is for the *Karmas* only for a good cause or social work, and whatever he gets from *Karmas*, he uses for his livelihood. The main component for successfully doing *Karma* is the place, doer (कर्ता), things needed for work, planning for the Karmas and lastly the fruits of action. The first four components, we can do it, but the last one is not in our hands, it is in the hands of Almighty, where He (परमात्मा) takes care of our past *Karmas* also into the account while giving the fruits of our actions. Therefore, Krishna advises Arjuna that never abandon your *Karmas* and your motive of *Karmas* should not be on the fruits of action. Your duty is only for the Karmas.

A student's duty or *Karma* is to study and write for the examination. Getting marks in the examination is not in his hands, but it is in the hands of the examiner. Therefore, don't snatch away the examiner's right to give marks. For doing any duty or *Karmas,* one has to follow some rules and regulations. If we don't follow it then it will be just like a machine rules us, and if we know the mechanism or rules of the machine, then we rule the machine. Therefore, knowing the rules of *Karma* is important for success. When a man does *Karma* or any duty without expecting any fruits of action, the greatest advantage is that his mind will be at peace. If a man does with a selfish motive, then he expects the fruits of action which is meant for him only. That way his egotism and pride increase. However, a man of wisdom does *Karmas* like a selfish man, but he dedicates the fruits of action to the almighty (*Ishwara*). He thinks the materialistic body is responsible for the *Karmas*, and he is just a mediator (actor) for the *Karmas.* Whatever benefits he gets for his *Karmas*, he dedicates to society or to the *Ishwara.*

If a man should not perform work prompted by desires for their results, how then should he perform it?

48. O Dhananjaya (Arjuna), give up attachment, considering failure and success as equal, perform actions steeped in Yoga. The state of being equable (in control of the mind) is called Yoga.

> "हे धनंजय आसक्ति का त्याग करते हुए और कर्म की सिद्धि हो या असिद्धि. दोनों को समान मानते हुए, योग में स्थित ही कर्म कर (कर्म के सिद्ध होने या निष्फल में रहनेवाली बुद्धि की इस) समता को योग कहते है I"

From this stanza onwards, we have an exhaustive discussion on the technique of *Karma*-Yoga as conceived by Krishna in his doctrine of action. A complete technique of how one can live a life as a truly inspired worker is explained here. 'Evenness of mind, the tranquillity of mental composure in facing all pairs-of-opposite' is defined here as YOGA. The term Yoga indicates a special condition of the mind in which it comes to neutral equilibrium, while on all the ebb and flow of life's tides. The instructions in the stanza advise us that desireless actions can be performed only when one gets completely established in Yoga. Not only is it sufficient that a true worker should act in the world being established in equipoise and equanimity, but should, amidst the changes in the world, also reinforce his attachment (*Sanga)* to the immediate fruit of actions.

It should be clear that the term 'attachment' (मोह) here means all factors against which Krishna has already warned us in the earlier stanzas, and has insisted that we must renounce them all, i.e. wrong imaginations, false expectations, day-dream about the fruits-of-actions, anxieties for the results and fears of the future calamities that have not yet appeared to threaten our lives. All these nerve-racking mistakes belong to the delusory ego-centre. When we analyse closely the stuff of which the ego is made up, we can easily find that it is a bundle consisting of the MEMORIES OF THE PAST, AND HOPES AND EXPECTATIONS FOR THE FUTURE. The dead moments that are no more constitute the past. The future is unborn and does not yet belong to us. To live in the ego, therefore, is to live either in the buried grounds of dead moments or in the womb of time where the future now rests. By indulging in all these preoccupations, we lose the immediate moments given to us to act upon, to strive, to earn and to achieve. It is this unintelligent squandering of the wealth of the present chances through our brooding and imaginations that is hinted at here.

Thus, in complete self-forgetfulness to get intoxicated with the activities undertaken in the present is to live vitally, fully and entirely with all that is best in us. To dissolve ourselves thus-our past, our future, our hopes, our fears – into the fiery content in the present is to work in inspiration. Inspired work promises the greatest returns.

Karma-Yogi does the work without any selfishness, and he does the work for others only without expecting the fruits of action. For doing his *Karmas*, he has a place or an Institution for activities. While doing his *Karmas*, he builds an attachment with the *Karma* and for the place or the Institution. Due to some unavoidable circumstances, if he is asked to leave the place or the institution, he will be disturbed or unhappy in that situation. Therefore, Krishna advises *Karma*-Yogi not to have an attachment with a particular *Karma* or to the institution, then only he will be a perfect *Karma*-Yogi. For example, a scientist is working in the institution without any selfish gain because of his interest after his retirement. He is working for the institution or for a scientific invention. And he has built an attachment with the invention and with the institution. If he is asked to leave the institute, then he will be mentally disturbed and very unhappy. That means the scientist is not a true *Karma*-Yogi. A true *karma*-Yogi will have no attachment with the *Karma* and the institution, and for the fruits of action. That means we should not be intoxicated (नशा) by the *Karma* itself.

We may think the *Karma*-Yogi's characteristics are just like a machine, or car or a cycle. As we know, the machine or car does not have any ego. When the car reaches its destination, it does not feel happy or unhappy, or it does not expect any reward after reaching its destination, just like a true *Karma*-Yogi. Does it mean *Karma*-Yogi should work like a machine? In the machine or in the *Karma*-yogi, the *Karmas* is to be done by the materialistic components like the mind, sense-organs or the action organs and similarly in the machine also. But the main difference is in the *Karma*-Yogi, the materialistic components are driven by inner-consciousness (*Atama)*, which is non-perishable, whereas in the machine (car) again, it is driven by materialistic components only (fuel). Therefore, the *Karma*-Yogi has feelings and satisfaction, etc. If a car is driven by an ego-centric man, he takes all the credit for himself and for being unsuccessful, he blames the car or something else.

49. Far lower than the YOGA-of-wisdom is action, O Dhananjaya, seek thou refuse in wisdom; wretched are they whose motive is in 'fruit'.

"चूंकि हे धनंजय, बुद्धियोग की अपेक्षा कर्म बहुत ही छोटी श्रेणी का है, इसलिए तू इस बुद्धि की शरण जा I जो लोग केवल फल के उद्धेश से कर्म करते है, वे दीन होते है I"

This shloka has been defined by different authors in different ways. The '*Buddhi*-Yoga' means the *Karmas* done by intelligence. The *Karmas* (action) can be done in two ways, one way is to do *Karmas* with intelligence without expecting the fruits of action and doing actions with equanimity in mind, in success and failure in result, and called the *Buddhi*-Yoga. And another way is doing *Karmas* with the aim of the fruits of action. Here, Krishna tells Arjuna that the one who does the *Karma* is poorer than the *Karma* done by *Buddhi*-Yoga (*Karma* with intelligence), therefore, seek in *Buddhi*-Yoga. In shloka (2-41), the *Buddhi*-Yoga is also called practical *Karmas* with evenness in mind. Generally, *Sattvic* people do the *Karmas* with *Buddhi* (intelligence), and they get rid of sin in their life, and secondly, they treat the poor and rich in the same way. In short, *Buddhi*-Yoga is far superior to ordinary *Karmas*. The only thing one has to do in *Buddhi*-Yoga is do your duties without expecting the fruits of action and with evenness of mind. If one gets fruits with this nothing wrong with it.

Now learn what result he gains who performs his duties with evenness of mind.

50. A person endowed with wisdom gives up both good and bad deeds in this world. Therefore, adhere to Yoga. Yoga is dexterity in acting (it provides means to gain freedom from the bonds of action).

"समबुद्धियुक्त निष्काम कर्म-योगी इस लोक में पुन्य और पाप दोनो से अलिप्त रहता है। इसलिए तु इस योग का आश्रय ले I पाप-पुन्य से बचकर कर्म करने की कुशलता या युक्ति को ही योग कहते है I"

The main advice in this shloka is to do the planning well for the *Karmas* and keep your mind in evenness (समबुद्धि) while doing or after finishing the *Karmas* that is called *Buddhi*-yoga.

The *Geeta*, throughout this section, is sincerely calling upon man not to live on the outskirts of his personality, which is constituted of the worlds of sense-objects, the physical body and the mind, but to enter the realm of the intellect and from there to assert his natural manliness. Man is the supreme creature in the kingdom of the living beings because of the rational capacities of his discriminative intellect. As long as man does not utilise this special equipment within him, he cannot claim his heritage as a man.

After dissecting this stanza, we come to understand what exactly the Lord's intention is. When Yoga, which is the art of working without desire pursued, the *Karma*-Yogi becomes detached from all existing *Vasanas* within himself, both the good and the bad. The inner equipment that has become peaceful and serene is called *Antakarna* (अन्तकर्ण), which is unavoidable prerequisite for consistent, discriminative self-application in meditation (self-thinking). Thus, all actions when properly pursued become a means for the ultimate end of realising the *Atman* (self) through meditation, with a pure mind.

Ordinary people, who cannot discriminate between the doable and the undoable actions, are engaged in actions and are always seeking the fruit of their labours. This results in feverish activity to gain material benefit, which ultimately lands them in sorrow, suffering and unhappiness. We see all around us. In the pursuit of material well-being, people have neglected their spiritual being. When they succeed in their endeavour, they feel happy, but this feeling is transitory. More often, when they fail to achieve their desired goal or when they cannot hold the acquired gain, they are steeped in despondency and misery. For them, it is difficult to accept defeat in a sportsman-like manner so that they can start afresh with a clean slate and with renewed vigour.

Why should we cultivate the evenness of mind and consequently an extra dexterity (skill) in action?

51. The wise men with equanimity of mind, as a result of abandoning the fruit of action and acquiring freedom from the bonds of birth, reach the state where there is no unhappiness.

"समत्वबुद्धि से युक्त मनीषी लोक कर्म से उत्पन्न होनेवाले फल को त्यागकर जन्मरूप बंधन से हमेशा के लिए मुक्त हो जाते है तथा दुःखरहित स्थान को ही प्राप्त होते है I"

In the last shloka, we have seen the characteristics of *Buddhi*-yog. The Yogi, who keeps his mind evenness (समत्व) in success and failure, in favourable and unfavourable conditions and thinks about any problem through his inner consciousness. Then who is a man of wisdom (अनायम)? A man is a *Buddhi*-Yogi (intellectual), who does not concentrate on the fruits of action and who controls his mind and senses (मनीषी). However, wisdom stays when a man does his *Karmas* regularly but gives his fruits of action to needy people or to society, after fulfilling his needful desires for day-to-day activities. Let us take one example of a farmer. He does his *Karmas* regularly, sowing, growing and then harvesting it. Whatever he gets from the field, he keeps the food material for his use and the rest of the things he gives to the needy people or to society. We are talking, regarding a-man-of-wisdom; therefore he cannot do any wrong things like *Rassjic* or *Tamssic* people. But there is one danger of egotism. Because he does the *Karmas* through *Buddhi* (intellect), and whatever earnings (fruits of action) he gets, he gives to the needy people; therefore, he may get the egoism for giving to others, that danger he has to control through his wisdom. Krishna tells Arjuna that a man who has these three qualities of *Buddhi*-Yoga, who gives his fruits of action to the needy and who controls his senses and mind, is fit for mortality (मोक्ष).

The Lord further explains to Arjuna why a true devotion to work, should act, and with perfect evenness of mind to achieve. The wise-meaning those who know the art of true living, undertake all work, maintaining in themselves the full evenness of the mind, and thus abandon all anxieties for the fruits of actions. These two conditions, under which the wise work, bring out the full picture of an individual who acts upon renouncing both ego and ego-motivated desires. When one works with neither the ego nor desires, one achieves *Vasana*-purgation. This is possible when one always has the Higher-Goal in view.

52. When your intellect crosses beyond the mire of delusion or attachment, then you shall attain indifference as to what has been heard and what is yet to be heard.

"जब तेरी बुद्धि मोह के कलुष (जाल) से पार हो जाएगी, तब तूने जो कुछ सुना है और जो कुछ सुनना चाहता है, उस सब से विरक्ति (छुटकारा) हो जाएगी I"

The main problem for *Buddhi*-Yogi (intellect) is the attachment (मोह). The *Buddhi*-yoga, you cannot get immediately, and it is not a material designation, but it is a mental condition where one has to do continuous practice. Generally, a man does duties for his bodily relations like family, relatives or friends with the fruits of his actions. For him, bodily relations are his own, and others are not his own. And whatever he heard or hears from others or from the literature, it is related to the fruits of his action and that too for his bodily relations. For developing *Buddhi*-Yoga, he has to develop the evenness (अनायम) in his mind. How is the evenness of mind obtained? When your mind is steady and not fluctuating, how does the mind become steady? When you don't indulge and are required to interference in family or bodily relations. When doesn't he have any attachment (मोह)? When he does not have any attachment, then he does his duties for others and for his family members with the same intensity. Whenever he hears or learns from literature about the fruits of actions, but makes his own decisions through his conscious mind. That means he has developed the evenness in his mind, resulting in the *Buddhi*-yoga (intellect). Therefore,

Krishna tells Arjuna that attachment is the main hindrance to developing *Buddhi*-Yoga.

53. When your intellect, though perplexed by what you have heard, shall stand immovable and steady in the self (आत्मा), then you shall attain Self-realisation.

> “जब अनेक प्रकार के वेदवाक्यो चे चकराई हुई तेरी बुद्धि अपनी
> चंचलता को खोकर समाधिवर्ति में स्थिर हो जाएगी,
> तब तुझे योग प्राप्त होगा I”

When one's intellect comes to a steady equipoise, and is undisturbed by any of the experiences that reach one through the five great archways of knowledge, then one is considered as attained *Buddhi*-Yoga, even while enjoying sensuous pleasures and while the sense organs are letting in a flood of stimuli – does not get at all disturbed within one's inner serenity and equipoise. Then in that case, your mind also does not get confused with the Veda and its teachings.

Qualities of a harmonised individual

Arjuna said:

54. What, O Keshava, is the description of him who has steady wisdom and who is merged in the super-conscious state? How does one of steady wisdom speak, how does he sit, how does he walk?

"अर्जुन ने पूछा – हे केशव I सम्मान्धी में स्थित, स्थितप्रज्ञ के लक्षण क्या है? वह स्थिर बुद्धिवाला पुरुष किस प्रकार बाते करता है, कैसे बैठता है, और कैसे चलता है ?

In the last few shlokas, we have learned the characteristics of evenness of mind (अनामय), *Buddhi*-yoga (intellect) and importance of controlling senses (मनीषी). We also know how the attachment (मोहा) is responsible for going away from *Buddhi*-Yoga. Now Arjuna wants to know the behaviour of a man of wisdom (स्थितप्रज्ञ), how he talks, how he behaves in the outer world. If we want to know such a man, then we have to analyse his outer behaviour only. Generally, a common man does *Karmas* because of the desires but a man of wisdom (स्थितप्रज्ञ) does not have any desires, then from where does he get the motivation for the *Karmas*? And what is the difference between a common man and a man of wisdom in behaviour?

The lord now points out those characteristic attitudes to realise a Saint-hood (स्थितप्रज्ञ)

The Blessed Lord said:

55. When a man completely casts off O Parth, all his desires of the mind are satisfied in the self *(Atama)* by the self, then he is said to be one of steady wisdom.

"भगवान बोले – हे पार्थ, जब व्यक्ति अपने में ही अपने द्वारा संतुष्ट होकर मन में बैटी हुई समस्त कामनाओ का त्याग देता है, तब उसे स्थितप्रज्ञ कहते है I"

Here Lord Krishna tells Arjuna that for a man of wisdom (स्थितप्रज्ञ) there are mainly two conditions, the first one is that he has to finish his desires and be satisfied in himself. There are different ways for different devotees (साधक) because of their inner mental makeup. For *Gyan-Yogi* (A-man-of knowledge), the desires (कामना) are different, where he attains wisdom by knowledge, thinking and consciousness. For *Bhakti*-Yogi, the desires are different, where he leaves everything to the chosen God. He works because of his (God's) wish; the success and failure are given to God. And for the *Karma*-Yogi, the desires are different, where he attains wisdom through *Karmas* through consciousness. However, to get wisdom (स्थितप्रज्ञ) state in any of these paths, the senses are well under control and ego, attachment, anger, and greed have to be a minimum level all the time. Therefore, each type of devotee has to control their desires and be satisfied in self (आत्मा). Even one can judge his wisdom-hood if he is satisfied in himself and he does not need any external materialistic things for his satisfaction. The wisdom state (स्थितप्रज्ञ) is the inner get-up of a person. The other person cannot judge his satisfaction. These desires cannot be eliminated in a day or two. It needs constant thinking and practice through consciousness. If a man is satisfied in himself, then he is somewhat successful in attaining the wisdom or स्थितप्रज्ञ.

This verse describes the characteristics of *Gyan*-Yogi, where the devotee always uses his inner consciousness for right and wrong actions. But *Bhakti*-Yogi always uses his Faith in the Almighty for any situation, whether the action is right or wrong. Therefore, mostly, such devotees go in blind faith, which is very dangerous. However, for both types of Yogis, *Sattvic Gunas* is the prerequisite condition.

56. He whose mind is not shaken up by advarsity, and who in prosperity does not hanker after pleasure, who is free from attachment, fear and anger, is called a Sage of steady Wisdom?

"जिसका मन दु:खो में उद्विग्न नही होता और सुखो के प्रति जिसकी स्प्रहा नष्ट हो चुकि है, ऐसे आसक्ति, भय और क्रोध से रहित व्यक्ति को स्थितप्रज्ञ मुनि कहा जाता है I"

In the following three shlokas, the external characteristics of a man of wisdom (स्थितप्रज्ञ) are mentioned and is called as *Muni.* The one who is a stable being, whose mind is undisturbed in sorrow and joy, who is unattached, fearless, and free of anger, is described as a *Muni.* About the emotions that must be minimal in the individual who is master in all situations, we are here potentially told only these: (a) attachment (मोह), (b) fear (भय) and (c) anger (राग).

When an object has charmed one to a point of deep attachment, then fear itself starts of losing the object; secondly, the individual attitude towards those that come between him and the object of his attachment is called ANGER. Anger is nothing but a feeling that arises within us because of our attachment to an object, towards an obstacle between ourselves and the object of our attachment; the anger thus arising in the bosom is directly proportional to the amount of fear one entertains or the scores of the obstacle holding one back from winning one's object of love. Anger, therefore, is only *Raga* for an object expressed at an obstacle that has come between us and the object of our desire.

Moreover:

57. For one, who without attachment is neither happy nor yields to aversion for whatever good or bad falls to his lot, his wisdom is well balanced.

“जो व्यक्ति सभी विषयों में आसक्ति (attachment) रहीत है, जो अच्छा या बुरा कुछ भी प्राप्त होने पर न तो आनंदित होता है, न विरक्ति का बोध करता है, उसका ज्ञान प्रतिष्ठित हुआ है अर्थात वही स्थितप्रज्ञ है I”

Detachment from the world outside must equally be accompanied by growing balance in ourselves to face all the challenges in life. A mere detachment in itself is not the way of perfect life, in as much as it is only a negative existence of constantly escaping from life. To live in ATTACHMENT is to live in slavery to the things of the world. But the perfect one is HE who, with divine freedom, lives in the world, dexterously (with skill) meeting both joys and sorrows which life may provide for him. In winter, to be out under the sun and lie in its rays is to enjoy its warmth and simultaneously suffer its glare. To complain of the glare is to bring sorrow into the enjoyment of the warmth. One who is intelligent will either try to ignore the glare and enjoy the warmth fully or will shed the glare and bask in the enjoyable warmth. Similarly, life by its very nature is a mixture of both good and bad, and to live we must always adjust ourselves, avoiding the bad and striving to linger in the experience of the good. A man of wisdom (स्थितप्रज्ञ) experiences the best and worst in life with equal detachment because He is ever established in the true and the ETERNAL, which is the very self (*Atama*).

Moreover:

58. When a person withdraws his senses from the objects of senses as a turtle withdraws its limbs from all sides within itself, his wisdom is said to be well balanced.

जैसे कछुआ अपने अंगो को भीतर सिकोड़ लेता है, वैसे ही जो अपनी समस्त इन्द्रिया को इन्द्रिय-विषयों से खीचकर भीतर समेट लेता है, उसकी प्रज्ञा प्रतिष्ठित है I”

After explaining that a perfect-one (a) he is ever satisfied in the self (*Atama)*, Lives in perfect equanimity in pleasure and pain, and (c) has within Him a complete absence of attachment to rejoicing or any aversion, it is here mentioned that a man-of-wisdom has special knack for withdrawing his senses from all disturbing ‘field-of-objects’. The simile used here is very appropriate. Just as the tortoise can, even at the most distant suggestions of danger, instinctively withdraw all its limbs into itself and feel safe within, a man of perfection can consciously withdraw all his antennas that peep out through his five arches of knowledge called the sense-organs (organs-of-perception). In short, if a situation around him is disturbing or a bad condition and nobody listens or cares for him, then he goes into isolation but does not run away and keep his wisdom (स्थितप्रज्ञ) state intact just like a tortoise withdraws its limbs from all sides and remains safe.

The senses of a man who has concurred or controlled but the taste or desires for the senses cease (remain) to exist. How do even the senses-objects (taste) finally end? Listen:

59. The object of the senses turns away from the abstinent man, leaving the longing (behind); but his longing also leaves him upon seeing the supreme?

"निराहार रहनेवाला देहाभिमानी जीव के इन्द्रिय-विषय तो निवृत हो जाते है, पर उनके प्रति रस या आसक्ति रह जाती है I किन्तु परमतत्व का साक्षात्कार कर लेने पर उनका यह रस निवृत हो जाता है I"

We can observe cases wherein an individual comes to maintain sense-withdrawal from the sense-objects due to some physical incapacity or due to some mental mood of temporary sorrow or misery. In all these cases, though the sense-organs come to feel an aversion to the respective objects, their inclination for these objects merely remains dormant for the time being. Similarly, Arjuna doubts that even in a Yogin, the capacity to withdraw from the temptation of the sense-world may be temporary, and that under favourable or sufficiently tempting conditions, they may again raise their hoods to hiss to the poison.

But although the sense-objects may temporarily seem to turn away from him who is abstinent, the deep taste for them that is ingrained in his mind is very difficult to erase completely. Here, Krishna in his supreme wisdom assures the seeker that these impressions of sensuous lives that were lived in the past by the ego from the beginning of creation until to date, will all be erased, or at least made ineffective, as roasted seeds, only when the seeker transcends the ego and comes to experience the *Atma* (self).

60. O Kaunteya (Arjuna), these unruly and powerful sense organs of even a man of wisdom, who is striving to control them, robs his mind forcibly.

“हे कोन्तेय, यद्न्शील बुद्धिमान पुरुष के मन को भी मध देनेवाले बलवान इन्द्रिया बलपूर्वक विषयों में खीच लेती है I”

As indicated in the Shloka 59, sense-organs are very strong to take away the mental peace even in the man of wisdom (स्थितप्रज्ञ). However, the sense-organs can become weak if one does fasting (निरहारी), but as soon as fasting or due to disability of the sense-organ becomes normal, again the sense-organ robs (snatch away) the mental peace. For example one has a music listening habit, when his ears have a problem, he may lose interest in listening to music. As soon as his ears are normal, he goes back to his old habit of listening to music. Secondly, the sex sense-organ is one of the dominant factors. Even a man-of-wisdom can fall prey. Such examples are there in history and in day-to-day life. Once, Swamy Vivekananda gave a spiritual lecture in America, and after his lecture, one lady came to his room and asked him I want a child from you. Then Swamy told her, “Why can’t you adopt me as your child?” That is the characteristic of wisdom who has controlled his senses.

Invariably, among those who are practising the path of perfection (or religion), the common cause by which many true seekers fall away from the path is the same all over the world. After a few years of practice, they no doubt come to live in a certain inexplicable inward joy. Then, being overconfident and often even vain of their progress, they relax in their path (*Tapas*). Once they come back to the field of the senses, the turbulent senses violently snatch away from the poise of perfect meditation. Therefore, the Lord indicates the practice method by which he should struggle hard, in order to reach the eminence of perfection as a man of steady wisdom.

61. Therefore, a striving individual, controlling his senses, should sit poised and concentrate on me. Only wise is the steady who has control over his senses.

"अतएव उन सब इन्द्रियों को सयंमित करके, समाहित चित होकर, मेरे परायन हो अवस्थित रहे; क्योकि जिसकी इन्द्रिया वस में होती है, उसी की बुद्धि प्रतिष्ठित होती है I"

Since the sense-organs are thus saboteurs in the kingdom of the SPIRIT THAT BRING THE DISTARIOUS DOWNFALL OF THE EMPIRE OF THE SOUL. Arjuna is warned here that as a seeker of self-perfection, he should constantly struggle to control his sense-organs and their mad lustful wanderings in their respective fields. According to the West, to control is to suppress. No science of mental life can accept that suppression is psychologically healthy. But the Vedic theory is not pointing to any mental suppression at all. It is only advising an inward blossoming, an inner growth and development by which one's earlier fields of enjoyment through the senses drop out to make room for the perception of a new field of ample joys and more satisfying Bliss.

No one who, with excessive force, controls his *Indrriyas* (senses) by sheer strength of will and a sense of abstinence has any chance of flowering into a full-blown spiritual beauty. He who has all his sense-organs of their own accord, lying tamely surrendered at his feet, and who discovered the infinite perfection in himself, is called a man of perfection. Neither has he ruined his instrument of cognition, nor has he closed down the arches of knowledge in him due to discrimination (reasoning) power of knowledge as the sense-organs are never satisfied permanently. A perfect one is he whose sway over the animal within is so complete that the inner Satan has become for the sage in him a tame Caliban (slave) to run and serve faithfully.

Now the Lord, Krishna, proceeds to point out the source of all evil in the case of the unsuccessful.

62. A person contemplating the objects of the senses acquires attachments to them. Attachments lead to desire (for their satisfaction). And from any hindrance in fulfilling the desire, give anger.

"विषयों का चिंतन करते रहने से मनुष के मन में उनके प्रति आसक्ति पैदा होती है I आसक्ति चाह को जन्म देती है और चाह पूरी न होने से क्रोध उत्पन होता है I"

63. Anger leads to indiscrimination; indiscrimination results in memory loss (intelligence); confused memory gives rise to destruction of wisdom, and he perishes.

"क्रोध से चित में मोह उत्पन होता है और मोह से विभ्रम पैदा होता है I स्म्रति के लोप से उचित-अनुचित का विचार करनेवाली बुद्धि नष्ट हो जाती है और बुद्धि के नाश से स्वयं मनुष का ही नाश हो जाता है I"

The ladder of fall is very beautifully described here. The path of destruction for a seeker is so elaborately detailed in these stanzas that, fallen as we are, we shall know how to get back to our pristine glory and inward perfection.

Like a tree which emerges from a seed, the source of all evil starts from our own wrong thinking or due to imagination. Thought is creative; it can make us or mar us – if rightly harnessed, it can be used for constructive purposes; if misused, it can totally destroy us. When we constantly think about a sense-object, the consistency of that thought creates within us an attachment to the object of our thought. When more and more thoughts flow towards the object of attachment, they crystallise to form a BURNING DESIRE for the possession and enjoyment. The same force of the motion when directed towards the obstacles that threaten the non-fulfilment of our desires is called ANGER (क्रोध). An intellect fumed with anger comes to experience DELUSION, and the deluded intellect has no power of discrimination, because it loses all the memories of the past. Once this 'consciousness' is dulled, the man becomes a two-legged animal. Anyone who is filled with anger is capable of doing acts while totally forgetting himself and his relationship with others. Sri Shankaracharya says in this connection that a deluded fool who is in this mental condition might even fight with his own teachers and parents while forgetting his indebtedness to these revered persons.

The contemplation (planned) of sense-object has been described as the source of all evils.

Let us take an example of an eye-sense. There are two places near your neighbourhood. One is a dirty place and another is a beautiful garden. The eye's function is to see both places. Once you leave these places, and if you like the garden, then you will have an attachment or desire to visit the garden daily. One day, if a gardener objects to you not coming into the garden, then because of your attachment or desire, you get angry. With anger, you fight with the gardener. Once anger enters your mind, the discrimination of intellect is lost and without knowing the reason, you fight with the gardener because of attachment and desire. Once your discriminating power is lost, you are ruined and become a four-legged man.

64. A self-controlled person whose senses are free from desire and hate attains tranquillity of mind even when moving in the objects of the senses.

> "परन्तु आसक्ति और विद्वेष से रहित होकर, सयमित मनवाला जो पुरुष अपने वश में की हुई इन्द्रिया के द्वारा विषयों में व्यवहार करता है, वह प्रसन्नता को प्राप्त होता है I"

He alone, who with perfect Self-control goes through life among the infinite number of sense-objects, each impinging upon him and trying to bind him with charm, and approaches them with neither love nor hatred, comes to enjoy PEACE. By running away from the sense-objects, nobody can assure himself any inner peace, because the inner peace depends upon the presence or the absence of the sense objects in the outer world, but essentially upon the mind's agitations for procuring the desired objects, or for getting rid of the undesired objects.

But a master of wisdom with perfect Self-control, moves among the objects of the world with neither any special love nor any particular aversion for them. Whenever I go, my shadow must play all around me according to the position of the light; but the shadow can either entangle me with love or destroy me with hatred. The outer world of objects is able to whip that man who lends the power to the objects to smother him.

When a mind is trained in following two aspects to (a) live in self-control, (b) move among the sense-objects with neither an attachment for, nor an aversion to them, the disturbances and agitations in the mind caused by the sense-enchantments are all immediately brought under control. This condition of the mind is called tranquillity or peace (प्रसाद).

What will happen when peace is attained?

65. Tranquillity of mind results in the destruction of sufferings, as the intellect of that tranquil-minded person soon attains equilibrium.

"इस प्रकार चित्त की प्रसन्नता प्राप्त होने से उसके समस्त दु:खो का नाश हो जाता है, इसलिए प्रसन्नचित व्यक्ति की प्रज्ञा शिग्र पूर्ण रूप से स्थिर हो जाती है I"

Lord Krishna explains to Arjuna why he should develop and maintain the tranquillity of the mind within himself. In tranquillity, all the sorrows are destroyed. A peaceful mind is significant for happiness. PEACE IS HAPPINESS or VICE VERSA. The least-agitated mind is proof against all sorrows in as much as sorrow is nothing but a state of agitation of the mind.

It is very well known that all desires (वासना) existing within an individual, who is facing life constantly, cannot be fully eradicated by him. The secret of doing so has been explained here by the Lord. Keeping the mind exposed to an atmosphere of tranquillity (प्रसादा), consciously brought about through an intellectual life of self-control, is the secret whereby all the *Vasanas* (desires) can get eliminated.

Who does not get knowledge?

66. A person with an uncontrolled mind does not possess sound wisdom; one without sound wisdom has no *Bhavana* (perception, thinking); and one who is bereft of conscious thinking has no peace. How can one who has no peace attain happiness?

> "जो व्यक्ति युक्त (जुदा हुआ) नही है, उसको ज्ञान प्राप्ति नही होती I आयुक्त व्यक्ति भावना भी नही कर सकता I भावना से रहित व्यक्ति को शान्ति नही मिलती और अशांत है, उसे सुख कैसे प्राप्त हो सकता है?"

Here is an explanation of why quietude of the mind is so often and so insistently emphasised in the literature explaining self-perfection. Unless the mind is quiet, the individual will have neither the intellectual leisure for the cultural self-development, nor the inner energy for constantly living spiritual perfections that a truly developed man yearns for. Unless there is tranquillity, there cannot be steadiness of intellectual applications to the problem of life. Without the self-evaluation of life and true observation with a clear discriminative analysis, we cannot have within us the required amount of devotion to self-knowledge.

Why is there no knowledge for the unsteady? Listen:

67. Just as a gale of wind overpowers a boat floating on water, so the mind of one who goes after the wandering senses overpowers his discrimination.

"क्योंकि विषयों में विचरती इन्द्रियों में से जिस किसी के पीछे-पीछे मन जाता है, वह उन (साधक) के विवेक को उसी प्रकार बलपूर्वक हरकर ले जाता है, जिस प्रकार वायु जल में नौका को हर लेती है I"

Just as a ship with sails up and the helmsman dead would be completely at the mercy of the fitful storms and reckless waves, will not reach any definite harbour but gets destroyed by the very tossing of the waves, so too, life gets capsized and the individual is drowned, if his mind is unanchored and left to be carried hither and thither by the uncertain buffets of passionate sense-storms. Therefore, the senses are to be controlled if man is to live a better and more purposeful life, designed and planned for enduring success.

The Lord now concludes by Re-affirming his statement:

68. Therefore, O mighty armed (Arjuna), only his wisdom is stable whose senses are under control from objects of the senses from all sides.

"अतएव, हे महावीर अर्जुन, जिसकी इन्द्रिया अपने विषयों से सब प्रकार रोकी हुई है, उसकी बुद्धि स्थिर है I"

In this stanza, Krishna reasserts to Arjuna the same proposition, "Life is Self-control alone is life of worth living" He alone is a man of wisdom (स्थितप्रज्ञ), rooted in joy and Bliss, who has completely restrained all his senses from their wild roaming among their sense-objects.

By destroying the sense organs (which are) roaming in the sense-objects does not mean that a man of self-development should destroy his capabilities for perception of the world outside, nor does it mean that he is the one who has been rendered incapable of enjoying life. Sense-debility (incapacity) is not a sign of better knowledge. It is only meant that the sense-objects filtering through the five arch ways of knowledge will not, in a perfect man, flood his mind to bring his chaos and destruction of his established inner peace and tranquillity.

The ordinary individual in his egocentric existence becomes victimised by the sense organs, while he who has conquered the ego and has transcended his matter-identifications comes to live in freedom and perfect control over the tyrannical sense organs.

To make this point clear, the Lord proceeds:

59. Where it is night for the being, the man of wisdom (स्थितप्रज्ञ) is awake; that in which all beings are awake, it is a night for the seers (*Munies*).

> “समस्त प्राणियों के लिए जी अवस्था रात्रि या अन्धकार-स्वरूप है, उस अवस्था में स्थितप्रज्ञ (जितेन्द्रिय) व्यक्ति जागता रहता है I और जिस अवस्था में साधारण व्यक्ति जागते रहते है, आत्मज्ञानी के लिए वह अवस्था रात्रि या अन्धकार स्वरूप है I”

Here two points of view, namely, of ignorance (night) and of the wise (day), are contrasted. The ignorant person never perceives the world as it is; he always throws his mental colour on the objects and understands the imperfections within his mind to be a part and parcel of the objects perceived. The world as viewed through a coloured glass plane must look coloured. When the colourful medium is removed, the world appears as it is.

The common man (materialistic) does not understand what is right and wrong. He cannot understand, related to the self (*Atamic*) issues or inner consciousness. On the other hand, the man of wisdom (स्थितप्रज्ञ) does not take interest in the materialistic issues. He does not understand why materialistic people take an interest in perishable things. If a common man tries to converse the materialistic things (संसारिक) to him (स्थितप्रज्ञ), he won't understand and does not take interest in such discussions. What Lord Krishna is trying to tell us for the common and egocentric people, whatever light (day) he sees is dark (night) for him. And for a-man-of-wisdom whom it is day to know the knowledge of self (*Atama*), for common or for egocentric people, it is the night, meaning no interest in self-knowledge.

The Lord says those who have abandoned desires and whose wisdom is steady can attain peace or Moksha.

70. Just as the water from various rivers enters the full and calm ocean without disturbing it, so also the desires do not disturb the tranquillity of a state of the mind. Such individuals attain peace, not those who are immersed in desires.

> "जैसे सभी और से जल से भरते रहनेवाले (फिर भी) अचल भाव से स्थिर सागर में नदिया (बिना सागर को उद्धेलित किए ही) प्रवेश कर जाती है, उसी प्रकार जिस (पुरुष) में सारी कामनाए प्रवेश कर जाती है, वही शान्ति को प्राप्त करता है, भोगो को चाहनेवाला नही I"

It is very well known that although millions of gallons of water reach the ocean through various rivers, the level of water in the ocean does not change. Similarly, even though an infinite number of sense-objects may pour in their stimuli and reach the mental zone of the perfect man through his five sense-channels, they do not create any commotion of flux within his bosom. Such an individual who always finds his own level, in spite of the fact that he is living amidst the sense-objects and with sense-organs unavoidably ever in contact with the objects, is called a man-of-perfection. Krishna asserts that such an individual alone can truly discover peace and happiness within himself.

The desires are mainly for materialistic things only, and change is the constant for the materialistic world. The common man with an egocentric mind is like a child. If a child is crying, then you give a toy he keeps mum, but again after some time the toy does not satisfy him and again starts crying, if you give some other toy, he again keeps mum. Similarly, materialistic desires never keep you in mental peace. This is only possible when you control your desires or stay with needful desires and which is a characteristic of a man of wisdom (स्थितप्रज्ञ), where he is perfectly in mental peace (शांतिपथ)

Who gets tranquillity

Now Krishna tells who attains peace?

71. He who abandons all desires and goes forward free from attachment, egotism, sense of I and mine and conceit attains peace and tranquillity.

"जो पुरुष समस्त कामनाओ को छोड़कर स्प्रहा (इच्छा या भावना), ममता (affection) और अहंकार से रहित ही व्यवहार करता है, वह शान्ति को प्राप्त होता है I"

Some commentators believe that these stanzas explain the path of renunciation, which are, in fact, not altogether ignored in the text of the *Geeta.* Since, as we said earlier, the second chapter is almost a summary of the entire Divine songs, it has to indicate even *Sannyasa*-Yoga (*Gyan*-Yoga), which will be explained later on, at length and hinted at different places during the entire length of *Geeta.* "Having conquered the mental agitation that was created by the pairs of opposites, fight the battle of life. An individual renounces all desires and has no attachments or longings, and it asserts that it is without any sense of I-ness or My-ness. The ego is the cause of the sense-attachments and longings. Where ego is not perceptible – as in sleep, there is no longing of desire in an individual, or at least they are dormant. In short, all our sufferings in the world are caused by our own egocentric misconceptions and consequent arrogance, which is characterized by our ever-multiplying demands for wealth and our endless desires.

Sankaracharya beautifully explains this point of view in his commentary that “A man of renunciation” who after entirely abandoning all desires, goes through life being content with the bare necessities of life, who regards not as his, even those things which are needed for mere bodily existence, who is not in vain of his knowledge – such a man of steady knowledge, who knows *Brahman,* attains peace (*Nirvana*), the end of all the misery of mundane existence (*Samsara).* In short, he becomes a man of wisdom (*Brahman*).

In short, for attaining peace, one has to abandon the desires (कामना) except the desires needed to support the body and secondly, he does the day-to-day activities (व्यवहार) without any attachments and without any affection (नमता). Lastly, his egotism he keeps at its minimum level by means of his knowledge.

This devotion of knowledge is further glorified as follows:

72. O Partha (Arjuna), this is the state of the man who has achieved *Brahman* (स्थितप्रज्ञ) and having achieved this state, he is not confused. One who is steeped in this state, even at the time of death, achieves supreme bliss.

"हे अर्जुन, यही ब्रह्मस्वरूप अवस्थिति है I इस अवस्था को पाकर मनुश्य संसार में फिर मोह-भ्रम में नही पड़ता I म्रत्यु के समय भी इस ब्राह्मी स्थिती में प्रतिष्टित रहकर वह ब्रह्म में लीनता को प्राप्त करता है I"

To renounce all desires is to destroy completely the last venture of one's ego. Renunciation of ego is not the state of dull, meaningless emptiness. Where the delusory ego has ended, the state of full knowledge or selfhood has dawned. To realise the *Atama* (self) in one's own bosom is to realise at once the *Atama* which is All-pervading and Eternal (*Brahman*). When the ego has ended, the consciousness is not known to be anything other than the ETERNAL, and as such, the knower of TRUTH in a brilliant self (*Atama*) and becomes self, and therefore, this state is called Selfhood (ब्रह्म-स्थिती).

A doubt may still arise that even after the realisation, we may again fall back into the delusion of the ego and come to suffer the Ego's world of imperfections and sorrows. To deny this tragedy, we have been told how, having realised the *Atama* (self) once, no more can the individual fall back into his ancient delusions. This experience of self need not necessarily take place in youthful days of one's life. Even in old age, even in the last moment of this embodiment, if a seeker can come to experience, even for a moment, this egoless state of tranquillity and poise, even a passing glimpse of the selfhood, it is sufficient to gain the *Bramic*-state (स्थितप्रज्ञ).

To work without attachment, desires, egoism and vanity (घमंड), ever established in perfect equilibrium in both success and failure, is to deny the ego its entire field of activity and unconsciously to assert the greater truth that is in the self (*Atama*). Thus, in technique, the *Geeta's Karma*-Yoga is not at all different from the Vedantic technique. But Arjuna got confused and perplexed because he took Krishna's words too literally, and therefore, in the following chapter, he expresses his mental confusion in the opening lines. The Lord, therefore, explains *Karma*-Yoga exhaustively in the next chapter.

Chapter - 3

The *Karma*- Yoga

Arjuna a victim of his own delusion and illusions, had completely surrendered to the Divine wisdom of his friend, Lord Krishna, the words of his charioteer were not fully appreciated by him, all at once. His mind was so much overwhelmed by sorrow that he could not decide upon the right line of action. He had, at first, resolved not to fight the war and had vigorously marshaled a set of impressive arguments in support of his decision. Therefore, Arjuna is still and naturally too, partial to his own decision. All through the second chapter Arjuna's intellect was trying to follow closely, the arguments of Krishna, mainly to find faults with them, if he could, or at least to seek in them some support for his own decisions.

Chapter 3, consists of Arjuna's question: why action is important (1-2), Krishna's reply: action is inevitable (3-8); work as a sacrifice (9-16), importance of desireless action (17-24), the way learned and ignorant approach action (25-32), futility of action against one's nature (33-35), Arjunas's question: why one sins his will? (36), the Lord's reply: desire and anger are real enemies (37-43).

Arjuna said:

1. O Janardhana, if you consider knowledge (*Gyana-Yoga by Sankhya*) superior to action, then why, O Keshava, do you ask me to engage in this terrible action?

"अर्जुन बोला – हे जनार्धन, यदि आपके मत में ज्ञान कर्म की अपेक्षा श्रेष्टकर है, तो हे केशव, आप मुझे ऐसे भयंकर कर्म में क्यो प्रव्रत कर रहे है?"

2. You are virtually confusing me with your perplexing advice. Tell me your considered opinion, following which I may attain the Supreme.

"आप परस्पर विरोधी मतवाले वचनों में मेरी बुद्धि को मोहित-सा कर रहे है । जिससे मै कल्याण को प्राप्त हो सकु, ऐसा एक मार्ग मुझे निष्चय करके बताऐ I"

Arjuna still believes that to fight against his cousins, teachers, and grandfathers is a terrible (घोर) action. He seems to have forgotten, or not to have understood at all, Krishana's words in the last chapter. Arjuna means to say that Krishna's arguments were supporting the path of Renunciation (ज्ञान) and yet they included an advice to Arjuna to undertake the great and terrible path of action.

Arjuna did not understand the advice of Krishna, on one side He asks him to do the *Karmas* and other side He praises the *Gyan*-Yoga or *Buddhi*-Yoga (wisdom or स्थितप्रज्ञ). He (Krishna) also says the *Karma*-Yoga (2-37, 38) is far inferior to *Gyan*-Yoga (2-49). Therefore, Arjuna is confused, which path is good for him. Krishna tells him to do the *Karmas* of war, and at the same time, he praises *Buddhi*-Yoga. Arjuna knows that war is a horrifying *Karmas* where a lot of sin, a lot of cruelty and a lot of sentiments are involved, then how can one get the wisdom in such acts (*Karmas*). Therefore, he wants a definite answer (advice) from Lord Krishna, which path, either *Karma*-Yoga or *Gyan*-Yoga (*Buddhi*-Yoga), is better for him?

Actions (*Karmas*) is inevitable

Lord Krishna gives the following reply to Arjuna's question:

The Blessed Lord said:

3. In this world, there is a two-fold path, as I said before, O sinless one, the 'path-of-knowledge' of the Sankhya and the 'path-of-action of the Yogi" *or Karma*-yogi.

"श्री भगवान ने कहा – हे निष्पाप अर्जुन, इस संसार में दो प्रकार के मार्ग या स्थिति मेरे द्व्वारा पहलेही बतलायी गई है – ज्ञानियों के लिए ज्ञानयोग की तथा कर्मयोगियो के लिए कर्मयोग की I"

To consider the path of action (*Karma*-Yogi) and the path of knowledge (*Gyan*-Yog) as competitive is to understand neither of them. They, being complementary, are to be practised serially one after another. Once the minimum requirement of life is fulfilled, selfless activity gives a chance to the mind to exhaust many of its existing mental impressions. Thus purified, the mind gains such a flight that it can steadily soar into the subtlest realms of meditation, and finally come to gain the experience of the transcendental Absolute.

Men fit for spiritual discipline fall into two distinct categories: the active and the contemplative (deep thinking) temperamentally, these two classes fall so widely apart, that to prescribe for both of them one and the same technique for individual development would be to discourage one section and ignore its progress. It has to show methods of self-development to suit the mental and intellectual temperaments of both these categories.

In *Karma*-Yoga, *Karma* (activity) is there, but in *Gyan*-Yoga (Sankhya) also there is also *Karma,* like reading discussions, thinking, etc., they are nothing but *Karmas* only. Similarly, in *Karma*-Yoga also there is *Gyan* (knowledge), like which *Karma* is to be done and which is to be abandoned (अकर्मा) or which *Karma* is to be restricted (विकरमा). These things are based on knowledge only. The only difference is in *Gyan*-Yoga (knowledge) thinking and in *Karma*-Yoga, physical activity is given more importance. The way (path) for *Karma*-Yoga and *Gyan*-Yoga is different. *Karma*-Yoga goes through a materialistic world (प्रवर्ती) for their families, society, etc.

Karma-Yoga is for the desires and creation of wealth, but it (*Karmas*) has to be done with *Dharma* (ethics) only. In *Gyan*-Yog (निव्रती), wealth and desires are not important, but only truth or reality is given the highest priority.

As mentioned in this Shloka, *Gyan*-Yoga and *Karma*-Yoga are independent. In *Gyan*-Yoga, the self (*Atama*), which is permanent, is more important, and in *Karma*-Yoga, the materialistic body is important. In *Karma*-Yoga, our mind or intellect has to be trained to concentrate on a single goal by doing the selfless *Karmas*. Generally, our mind or intellect's nature is that it wanders anywhere without restrictions; therefore, our intellect has to be made practical and single-pointed (व्यवसायात्मक बुद्धि) by *Karmas*. According to Adi Shankaracharyya, *Karma*-Yoga is not a separate path for the highest goal but a first step for attaining *Gyan*-Yoga, where one can make the mind peaceful by selfless *Karmas* and then only *Gyan*-Yoga can be attained.

Arjuna listened carefully to the advice of Lord Krishna and then thought of going for the *Gyan*-Yoga as there is no sin in this path. The Lord Krishna advises the following in the next stanza.

4. Not by non-performance of actions does man reach 'actionlessness; nor by mere renunciation does he attain 'perfection.'

"केवल कर्म का प्रारम्भ न करने से ही मनुष्य नैष्कर्म्य की अवस्था को नहीं पहुंचता, न ही कर्म का त्याग कर देने मात्र से सिद्धि को पाता है I"

By mere renunciation of action *(Sannyasa),* no one attains perfection. Running away from life is not the way to reach the highest goal of evolution. Through action, to a purification of the inner instruments (soul), applying which the seeker walks the path of knowledge to reach ultimately the spiritual destination of self-development is indicated in this stanza.

Here, Lord Krishna is trying to tell Arjuna that one cannot walk independently on the path of knowledge (ज्ञान-योग). First, he has to do *Karmas* and learn to do the good selfless *Karmas* to purify the inner equipment (mind). In such a state, his *Karmas* (actions) become renunciation-of-action (अकर्मिक) and attain peace in his mind. All his *Karmas* become non-binding on him. Generally, such persons are bachelors to avoid the *Karmas* related to the family (आश्रम-जीवन). Such a man is ready to know the imperishable self (*Atama*) and becomes a man of knowledge (*Gyanyogi or sannyasi*).

Man cannot reach the 'actionlessness state' (निष्क्रम्य) without doing the *Karmas.* There are two weaknesses, first is not to start the *Karmas* and second is to stop doing *Karmas* in between. With these weaknesses neither one can get an actionless state (निष्क्रम्य) nor the perfection in knowledge (सिद्धि).

A man can remain in following four states:

1. A man has a feeling of doing *Karmas* (doer ship or कर्तापन). If the desires are bad, he will be ruined, and if the desires are good he will progress in his life.
2. He has a feeling of doing *Karmas* (doer ship) but no desires. Such a man does the *Karmas* as a duty, and he does not take the fruit of action for himself but for others. He does the work for others only without any selfish motive. For such a man, the good *Karmas* done for others get attached and will have a feeling of doer ship (Ego), done for others.
3. The third category does not do any *Karmas* (doer ship) but only desires. Such a man in *Geeta* is called a hypocrite (मिथ्याचारी) and they are of *Tamssic* in nature.
4. These category people neither have a feeling of doing *Karmas* or any desires. In this category, a man can be mad or a man of wisdom (स्थितप्रज्ञ).

   A mad man does not do any *Karmas* nor does he have any desires. But the difference between the two is that whenever any situation arises, a man of wisdom does his *Karmas* and has a desire. Once the *Karma* of the aim of the work is finished, that *Karmas* does not get attached to him. His *Karmas* are just like a drop of water on the cloth, meaning that when it is wet, it is seen. Once it is dried, no water drop can be seen.

When do the *Gyanis* and *Karma*-Yogis become detached? Both of them first have to start the *Karmas* and should not abandon in between. But one should remember that there should not be any desire behind doing *Karmas*, otherwise there is an attachment behind the *Karmas* and ties with the doer ship (कर्तापन). However, the same work or *Karma* is done without attachment and doer ship, it becomes actionless (निष्क्रम्य). Now the question arises, what happens to both types of Yogis after attaining actionlessness (निष्क्रम्य)? The *Gyanis* gets knowledge (सिद्धि) in his chosen aim, and similarly the *Karma*-Yogi also. The *Gyan*-Yogis realises the importance of self (*Atama*) and does not have any *Karmas* to be done. However, he does only those *Karmas* which are needed to support his materialistic body, just like a tortoise, whereas *Karma*-Yogi might be doing very strong actions (*Karmas)* but without any attachment. His *Karmas* become *Akarmic* (actionless), which does not bind him.

5. Verily, none can ever remain, even for a moment, without acting; for everyone is made to act helplessly, indeed by the qualities born of nature *(PRAKRITI).*

कभी कोई क्षण भर के लिए भी बिना कर्म किये नही रह सकता, क्योकि प्रकृति से उत्पन गुण सबको विवश करके उनसे कर्म कराते रहते है I”

Man is ever agitated under the influence of the triple tendencies of Un-activity *(Sattva),* Activity *(Rajas)* and Inactivity *(Tamas)* inherent in him. Even for a single moment, he cannot remain inactive. Total inactivity is the character of insentient matter. Even if we are physically at rest, mentally and intellectually we are active all the time, except during the state of deep sleep. So long as we are under the influence of these three mental tendencies *(Gunas),* we are helplessly prompted to labour and to act.

Therefore, not to act at all is to disobey the laws of nature, which shall, as we all know, bring about a cultural distortion in ourselves. If there is a creature that remains inactive physically, he will get absorbed in his thoughts. Therefore, Krishna advises Arjuna to act vigorously with the RIGHT-ATTITUDE of mind, so that he may avoid all internal waste of energy and learn to grow in himself.

Human beings have the intelligence and the thinking power. They cannot sit ideally, although their action organs might be at rest, but their mind wanders here and there depending upon their *Gunas*. Therefore, *Parakriti* forces them to act. What about *Gyan*-Yogi and the *Karma*-Yogis who have already crossed the triple *Gunas*? Krishna says that they also do the *Karmas* whenever it is required, but the *Karmas* do not bind them. Once the *Karmas* are over, again they go to their previous states.

6. He who, restraining the organ of action, sits thinking in his mind of the sense-objects, he of deluded understanding, is called a hypocrite.

> "जो (हाथ-पैर आदि) क्रमन्द्रियो को रोककर मन से इन्द्रियों के विषयों का चिंतन करता रहता है, वह मूढ़ व्यक्ति मिथ्याचारी कहलाता है I"

A man who does not use his action-organs means no activities and sits only thinking about his-organs in his mind, is called a hypocrite (मिथ्याचारी). He is not doing any action, but mentally thinking and promoting lust for his sense-organs is a deluded fool. Such a man cheats himself and others.

7. But whoever, controlling the senses by mind, O Arjuna, engages his organ-of-action in *Karma*-yoga, without attachment, he excels.

> "किन्तु हे अर्जुन, जो (चक्षु-कर्नादी) ज्ञानेन्द्रियो को मन से संयम करके अनासक्त भाव से कर्मेन्द्रियो के दव्वारा कर्मयोग का अनुष्ठान करता है, वह श्रेष्ट है I"

In the last Shloka, characteristics of a hypocritical man were explained. In this Shloka, He (Lord Krishna) explains the characteristics of an excellent person (श्रेष्ठ-पुरुष) and says that he controls his sense-organs through his mind and directs his action organs for doing the

Karmas without any attachments. There are mainly three characteristics of such an excellent person. First is he controls his sense-organs, and whatever he wants to see or hear or talk is decided by his mind and not by the sense-organs' instincts. The second character is whatever work he gets rather, whatever work he wants to do, he will do whole heartily without expecting the fruits of *Karmas.* His work itself is the fruit of his actions. However, whatever he gets in his actions, he accepts it very gracefully. The third characteristic is that he does his *Karmas* with full heartedly, no laziness, and he sets an example in his own family and in society. Krishna tells Arjuna that you too should be like this (excellent person or श्रेष्ठ-पुरुष).

8. You perform bounden duty; for action is superior to inaction. Even the maintenance of the body would not be possible for you by inaction.

> "तू शास्त्रों-द्वारा निर्दिष्ट कर्म कर, क्योकि कर्म न करने की अपेक्षा कर्म करना श्रेष्ट है I फिर कर्म न करने से तेरी शरीर-रक्षा भी तो नही होगी I"

In our work-a-day world, we must understand this term 'bounden duty' (नित्य-कर्म) in the text, to include all 'obligatory actions' of the individual in his home, in his office and society as a national being. Thus, not to perform diligently all our duties in the home and in the world outside would be inaction. We are warned that even a healthy bodily existence is not possible if we were to live in complete inertia and inactivity. Inactivity brings about the destruction of society, and of the home, and often the very individual himself becomes victimised by his idleness and suffers physical debilities and intellectual deterioration.

In one of the stanzas in chapter 2, Lord Krishna says that knowledge is superior to *Karmas.* Therefore, Arjuna got confused and asked Lord clearly what is good for him, whether knowledge or *Karmas.* In this stanza, the Lord clearly tells Arjuna you do *Karmas* only. He (Lord) further says that doing *Karmas* is far better than not doing the *Karmas.* There are mainly four types of *Karmas.* The first one is the bounden duty (नित्य-कर्म). One has to do the regular daily *Karmas*, including cleaning work. You don't get any fruits of action by these *Karmas,* but if you don't do it, one can end in a great disastrous effect. In all walks of life, like farmers, teachers, doctors or cleaners etc, they have to do their bounden *Karmas* regularly. The second type of *Karma* comes on special occasions like festivals, natural calamities, or in any community functions, etc. The third type of *Karma* is desire-prompted actions, which generally egoistic and *Rajssic* people undertake. The fourth type of *Karma* is completely prohibited, like stealing, innocent killing, cheating, etc. Therefore, everybody does the *Karmas*, but Krishna advises Arjuna to do the bounden duty *Karmas.*

Work as a sacrifice

9. The world is bound by actions other than those performed for the sake of sacrifices; do thou therefore, O son of Kunti, act for that sake (for *Yajna)* alone, free from all attachments.

"यज्ञ के लिए किये गये कर्मों के शिवाय अन्य कर्मों से इस संसार में व्यक्ति कर्मबंधन से युक्त (बंधा) हो जाता है, अत: हे कौन्तेय, तू आसक्ति को छोड़कर यज्ञ के निर्मित कर्म कर I"

Every action does not bring about bondage upon the doer, such as *Yajnas. Yajana* here means "any self-sacrificing work, undertaken in a spirit of self-dedication, for the blessing of all. It is only unintelligent and selfish activities that thicken the impression in the mind, and thus successfully build a thick and impenetrable wall between the spirit (egocentric mind) and the unlimited Divine spark-of-life (*Atama*) in us. Every action motivated by egocentric desires thickens the veil and permits not even a single ray of essential divinity to peep through it, to illuminate the life in us. According to the traditional translation, all activities other than the *Yajna*-activities will bring about *Vasana*-bondages, and an individual's ultimate development and growth will be arrested.

In short, the *Karmas* which are done with sacrifice (यज्ञ) does not bind the person. Mostly, we do *Karmas* with the fruits of action; therefore, it binds us. Earlier in Chapter 2, Sholka 50 also it has been explained in detail how one has to conduct oneself for sacrificial *Karmas.* Now the question arises, this war for Arjuna, is it a sacrificial *Karma*? Yes, because if Duryodhana wins this war, then injustice (अधर्म) will happen and innocent people will suffer. Therefore, Krishna advises Arjuna that go ahead with the war as a sacrifice without having any attachment to the concerned people.

10. In the beginning of this age, *Prajapati* (ब्रम्हा, the creator) created mankind together with the *Yajna* and said, "By this (*Yajna)* you shall propagate and prosper and shall be the giver of desires (*Kamadhuk*) to you.

"सृष्टि के प्रारम्भ में प्रजापति ब्रम्हा ने यज्ञ के साथ प्रजा को उत्पन करके कहा कि इस यज्ञ के द्वारा तुम बुद्धि को प्राप्त होओं, यह तुम्हारे लिए अभीष्ट कामनाओ की पूर्ति करनेवाला बने I"

Even when the creator, total-mind, puts up the show of the Universe of the five elemental forces (Air, Water, Space, Ether, and Fire) and brings forth the living organisms along with the man, on this stage of life to work, to strive and achieve, he created also *Yajna* – the spirit of self-dedicated activities. The *Yajna*-spirit is seen everywhere, the sun shines, the moon appears, the sea throbs, the earth bears – all in the spirit of sacrifice and self-dedicated motherly love with never a trace of attachment of any kind of self-arrogating motive.

The whole world of cosmic powers and nature's phenomena function instinctively in the service of all. Even before life could appear on the face of earth, the elemental forces had prepared the field with their constant activities performed in the sacred spirit of dedication. Even when life develops and multiplies, at all levels, we can easily recognise different degrees of *Yajna*-activities, which keep up the harmonious growth of existence.

11. With this, you do nourish the Gods and may those *DEVAS* nourish you; thus, nourishing one another, you shall attain the highest Good.

"इस यज्ञ के द्वारा तुम देवताओ को पुष्ट करो और देवता तुम लोगोको पुष्ट करे I इस प्रकार परस्पर एक दुसरे का पोषण करते हुए परम कल्याण को प्राप्त होओंगे I"

The whole *Vedic* concept of *Devas* is that of one Universal power, ever active in the world of phenomena, receiving appropriate names because of its multiple functions, like Indra *Deva* is meant for giving the rain to the earth. All the *Vedic* Gods are but functional names of the supreme creative power manifesting in myriad (countless or many) forms.

It is obvious that the productivity that is dormant in any situation can be invoked only by men's sincere efforts. This potential, which generally lies dormant everywhere, and *Devas* to be cherished by the worker through the *Yajna* and certainly the *Devas* will manifest themselves to cherish or bless the worker. Thus cherishing one another, man shall gain the Highest Good, which is Divine intention in the mind of the creator, says Krishna in this verse.

12. The *Devas*, nourished by the sacrifices, will give you the desired objects. Indeed, who enjoys objects given by the *Devas*, without offering (in return) to them, is verily a thief.

"देवताजन यज्ञ से संतुष्ट और पुष्ट हो तुम लोगों को अभीष्ट भोग्य वस्तुए प्रदान करेगे I इसलिए उनके द्वारा प्राप्त भोगो को उन्हें बिना दिये जो भोग करता है, वह चोर ही है I"

He who enjoys objects, given by the *Devas* (Gods), the productive potential tapped, without offering his own *Yajna*-efforts (poor and needy people) into it, is termed here by Krishna as a social thief, considering the moral and ethical idealism recognized and respected at times in *Geeta*, the term 'thief' used here is indeed a powerful word, fully implying the low depravity and disrespectful nature of such a social criminal who eats without producing.

13. The righteous, who eat the 'remnants of the sacrifices', are freed from the sins; but those sinful ones, who cook food (only) for their own sake, verily eat sin.

"यज्ञ का अवशिष्ट खानेवाला सन्तजन समस्त पापो से मुक्त हो जाते है, किन्तु जो केवल अपने लिए पकाते है, वे पापिजन तो पाप ही खाते है I"

The people who receive for themselves their 'share' after sweating hard in sincere *Yajna*-activities (social activities), 'go beyond all sins'. Krishna seems to be against the principle of arrogation of wealth, and of hoarding the same, motivated by lust of lucre, meant mainly for selfish enjoyment, utterly regardless of the privations and poverty of the unfortunate folks around in the community. It is said that such hoarders of wealth 'eat but sin'.

For the following reasons, also, Action (*Karmas*) should be performed by someone who is qualified for action. For it is *Karmas* that sets the wheel of the universe moving. HOW? Answer follows:

14. From food come forth beings; from rain, food is produced; from sacrifices arises rain, and sacrifice is born of action.

"अन्न से प्राणी उत्पन होते है, अन्न की उत्पति मेघ से होती है I मेघ यज्ञ से होता है और यज्ञ कर्म से उत्पन होता है I"

15. Know that action comes from *BRAHMAJI* (the creator) and *Brahmaji* comes from imperishable. Therefore, the all-pervading *Brahman* (God-principle) ever rests in sacrifice.

“कर्म को वेद से उत्पन हुआ जानो और वेद को अक्षर से I इसलिए सर्व-व्यापी वेद नित्य यज्ञ में प्रतिष्ठित है I”

In this stanza, as also elsewhere all along the *Geeta*, the familiar terms of the Vedic period have been charged with new meanings and significance. Rain is an essential condition for the conversion of the mineral raw material into enjoyable and nutritious food. Similarly, in all fields of activity there is an enjoyable profit which can be gathered only when the fields come under ‘condition favourable’ for them to produce these profits. Self-dedicated activities (*Yajna)*, when performed in any given field of endeavour, will create the conditions necessary for the field to smile forth (rain) in a luxurious ‘crop of profit’, enjoyable by the society.

For example, the wasteful waters of a river flowing idly can be dammed and made use of; if the waters are intelligently employed in irrigation, the fertile lands now lying fallow on its banks. Through sacrifice and work a dam can be built, and when it is built, it provides ‘conditions helpful’ for bringing the lands on either side under the plough. Again, for making use of irrigated land, man has yet to strive; ploughing, sowing, weeding, waiting, gathering – before he can come to enjoy the profit of his activities – the food.

We are shown how this wheel-of-action (stanza 15) is connected with and includes the Supreme. The principle of right action, even the power to act, has come out of the creator himself, and the creator is none other than the Imperishable Supreme. Action is in the newborn live-baby; action is the gift from the creator! Therefore, the All-pervading Supreme is ever centred in all undertakings pursued, by one or many people, in an honest spirit of self-dedication, for the good of all.

He, who lives in unison with this wheel of action, is contributing to the harmony of life. What happens to him who disobeys the unison with the wheel of action?

Importance of Desireless Actions

16. He who does not follow here the wheel thus set revolving, is of a sinful life, rejoicing in the senses. He lives in vain, O son of Partha!

> "जो इस लोक में इस प्रकार प्रवर्तित यज्ञ-चक्र के अनुसार व्यहार नही करता, वह पापी और इन्द्रियारम है तथा व्यर्थ ही जीवन-धारण करता है I"

Every member in the entire kingdom of minerals, the vegetables and the dump-creatures, instinctively follows the principles of *Yajna* (meaning sacrifices) and contributes thereby to the smooth running of the Universal wheel-of-action. Among living creatures, man alone has been allowed the FREEDOM OF ACTION to contribute to the harmony, or to bring about discord in the smooth running of this cosmic mechanism. So long as the majority of a generation manages to live abiding by the law of Harmony, they shall grow from strength to strength, opening up fields of happiness for themselves. Such periods are called the Golden eras of their social and cultural life.

But this faithful obedience is not always possible for all of them at all times. At certain periods of history, man, as a social being, comes to revolt against this Eternal Law, and then, life starts slipping away from its peaceful domain of constructive growth, and shatters itself in tearful ruin. Such ages are the dark ages of despair and restlessness, war and pestilence, flood and famine.

In such an era, nobody would come forward to work in the redeeming noble spirit of *Yajna*, without which, no 'favourable circumstances' (rain) could be created for the 'productive potentials' to manifest themselves as nourishing joy. Seekers of senses (इन्द्रिया-रमह), they compete among themselves, each seeking with lustful greed his selfish happiness, and they often, unconsciously, bring about a discordant rhythm in the wheel of action. Such people are considered by the *Geeta* as 'living in sin', and the Divine song asserts, 'they live in vain'.

How can a wheel-of-action (sacrifice) be followed by the ज्ञान-योगी (a man of knowledge)?

17. But the man who rejoices in the self (*Atama*), who is satisfied with self, who is content in the self alone, for Him verily there is nothing (more) to be done.

"परन्तु जो व्यक्ति आत्मतत्व में ही रमत करनेवाला है और आत्मा में ही तृप्त तथा आत्मा में ही संतुष्ट है, उसका कोई कर्तव्य नही है I"

As mentioned in Chapter 2, Lord Krishna has described two paths for the highest evolution for human beings. One is knowledge (ज्ञान) and another is *Karmas* (action), depending upon the mental get-up of the individual, which also comes from past life. However, in the beginning, both have to do the निष्काम *Karmas* to make the mind at peace (evenness). *Nisshkam Karmas* (निष्काम-कर्मा) means selfless actions. Then afterwards *Gyanis* goes or tries to acquire more knowledge, regarding the self (*Atama*) and *Karma* -Yogi continues to do the *Karmas*. *Gyani (Sannyasi)* learns the functions of mind and materialistic body and self and realises that this world (संसार) is apparent (मिथ्या), then slowly and slowly his actions (*Karmas*) are dropped. Such a *Gyani* does not do any *Karmas* and is satisfied in the self (*Atama*) itself. Once he becomes a man of wisdom (ज्ञानी) how his

Karmas are dropped, and he does not do any actions as explained below.

The wheel of action explained above is generally applicable to the majority of seekers. But the actions in the world undertaken in the spirit of *Yajana* integrate their personality and make them more and more prepared for the highest vocation in life, meditation. Through selfless work, an individual gains an increasing amount of inner poise and when such a single-pointed mind is brought to function at the meditation seat, the meditator gains the experience of transcending his limited ego. To such a perfected one, work is not a training to purify himself, but it is a fulfillment of his own God-realization.

It is a fact that we are egged on to activity seeking and demanding a better SATISFACTION and a complete CONTENTMENT. Satisfaction and contentment are the two wheels of the life-chariot. To gain a better satisfaction and to reach nearer the point of contentment, we are goaded to act in the outer world (संसार), to earn, to save, to hoard, to spend. But the man-of-perfection (ज्ञानी), who on transcending his limited identification with matter-envelopments, when he gets himself ushered into All-perfect Realm of the spirit, he comes to feel so satisfied with the state of self-hood which he thereby attains, that he experiences a complete sense of contentment in the very Divine Nature and that provides eternal satisfaction for him.

Where satisfaction and contentment have arrived in that bosom, desires cannot arise at all, and where the desires are not, there cannot be any action. Naturally, in such an individual, there cannot be any 'obligatory duties; all work has been at once fulfilled in him. Thereafter, he is free to act or not to act, to serve or not to serve and lives as a God-man on the earth, guiding the people in the right direction.

18. For him (*Gyani*), there is no interest whatsoever in what is done, or what is not done, nor does he depend upon any being for an object.

"उस ज्ञान-निष्ट व्यक्ति का इस संसार में न तो कुछ करने से प्रयोजन है और न नही करने से ही I इस मनुष्य का समस्त प्राणियों में कोई भी मतलब अटका नही है
(अर्थात उसका संसार में किसी से कोई लेना-देना नही है) I"

In the entire chapter, these two stanzas are related to the ज्ञानी-पुरुष (a man of wisdom) where his *Karmas* are dropped and he is not dependent on anybody. However, attaining this *Gyani*-state is not child's play and very difficult, where first he has to attain evenness in mind by developing the सात्विक (pure) qualities in his personality. In this state, his ego, attachment, desire, anger, etc. are at their minimum level. Then he concentrates on the self and develops the qualities where he is satisfied in the self (आत्मरति), attached with self (आत्म-तृप्ति) and content in the self (आत्म-संतुष्टि). He realises that self (आत्मा) is a part of the Almighty (ईश्वर), therefore, he considers all living beings to be part of the Almighty and treats them with affection, including the Almighty's nature (प्रकर्ति). However, he does the differentiation based on intelligence (बुद्धि). For example, if he is asked to choose or protect between a dog and a man. He chooses man because of his intelligence, or between *Sattvic* (सात्विक) and *Tamssic* (तामसिक), he chooses the *Sattvic* man. Therefore, in this stanza, it is indicated that a *Gyani* spends his life only in the service of Almighty, means for others whenever or whatever his services are required. In this state, he (*Gyani*) need not do any rituals or religious prayers. He is above in all such things.

An ordinary man is whipped up to action either because of his anxiety to gain profit or because of his fear that by not doing work, he will incur a loss. But an individual, who has the minimum requirement for life existence, and who has the subjective experience of the spiritual stature in him, who has, therefore, discovered an Eternal satisfaction in his own self (*Atama*) and who has reached perfect contentment therein, will have no more action to perform. He has nothing more to gain through activity, nor can he have any fear of losing anything in the world due to non-performance of any action. Such an individual, rooted in the experience of the self, and depending upon nothing – neither any being nor any object – for his joy and Bliss, has discovered the subject; the objects of the world are essentially nothing other than the 'subject' being tossed on the waves of agitations in the mind.

In your case (Arjuna), you are not still in this state of mind (ज्ञानी).

19. Therefore, always perform the action which should be done, without attachments, for by acting without attachment, man attains the Supreme.

"इसलिए तू अनासक्त होकर सदैव अपने कर्तव्य-कर्म सुचारू रूप से करता रह, क्योंकि आसक्ति छोड़कर कर्म करता हुआ मनुष्य परम पद को पा लेता है I"

Till now, Krishna was explaining the wheel-of-action, and after exhausting the exposition of this entire theory, he, in this stanza, is crystallising his conclusions, encouraging Arjuna to act. Always perform actions which are obligatory in your present social status, in your domestic situation, as a member of your community and nation. Even here, Krishna is repeating his warning to Arjuna that he must be careful in all his activities, to keep his mind away from all dangerous attachments. The Lord has already explained how 'attachment' directly helps to form tendencies in the mind and deepen fresh *Vasana*-impressions within.

Man is not tied by *Karmas* (actions), but tied by his desires for fruits. Desires only destroy the man and not by the *Karmas. Karma* done without desires (attachments) and done for the others liberates the man and gets rid of attachments. *Karmas* mean actions, and *Karma*-Yoga means peace. The actions done for materialistic needs of the body are called *Karmas*. And the actions done for others are called *Karma*-Yoga, which gives peace in the mind and self (*Atama*).

The following four points are to be kept in mind while doing *Karmas,* which will take you to reality and the highest position.

1. Detachment (अनासक्त-होकर) – While doing actions, don't be attached to actions and fruits should not be the motive.

2. Always (सर्वदा) – Don't stop the actions in between and do always until it is finished.

3. Duty (कर्तव्य) – Your duty towards family, society and nation to be kept in mind.

4. Ethics (आचरण) – Keep the ethics while doing *Karmas* and think through consciousness while undertaking any actions.

One more reason to fight in this war.

20. Janaka and others attained perfection verily through action alone; even to protect the masses, you should act.

"सच पूछो तो जनक आदि कर्म के द्वारा ही सिद्धावस्था को प्राप्त हुए है I लोकसंग्रह को देखते हुए भी तुम कर्म ही करने योग्य हो I"

The wise king of yore, such as Janaka, had tried to attain perfection (समसिद्धि) by the path of perfection. They were men of right understanding as they tried to liberate themselves through right actions performed in a spirit of detachment and self-dedication. They had set an example to the world by their achievement through an immaculate (perfect) life of service. Krishna means that Arjuna, too, is a prince by birth, and one who has taken upon himself the entire responsibility of mobilising and fighting the war. He had a greater responsibility towards the community than any other member. Therefore, it was his duty that he should keep to his post and work diligently.

Krishna tells Arjuna that the king Janaka attained Moksha (immortality) by doing *Karma*-Yoga, and he was not a *Gyan*-Yogi (*Sannyasi*). Seeing your past *Karmas* (प्रबध-कर्मा), you are born in the family of royal kings. Therefore, by doing actions, you can become *Karma*-Yogi by doing right actions for the community, and you can also attain immortality (मोक्ष) without becoming *Gyan*-Yogi (*Sannyasi*).

As explained above, Lord Krishna had given the example of King Janaka and asked Arjuna to follow him for *Karma*. This is not only applicable for Royal families but also applicable for the common people when one does the actions without any attachments (अनासक्त). The attachment (आसक्ति) can be of two types: I-ness (Ego) for the *Karmas* (कर्मासक्ति) and secondly, *Karmas* for the fruits of action (फलासक्ति or भोक्तापन). If a man Surrenders (समर्पण), these two aspects to the Almighty (ईश्वर), then I-ness and anxiety for the fruits of action go away. If we consider God as an instrument for these two aspects and work like a worldly person (संसारिक), then the action does not remain like a worldly person. The I-ness is dropped, and he works for his family or for others with the same intensity. The question may arise if it is not meant for us, then how does the motivation come for doing actions? This question cannot be answered by logic but through a spiritual mind (अध्यात्मिक) only, and can be experienced by oneself. This type of *Karmas* is nothing but *Karma*-Yog, like a *Gyan*-Yog and can attain the highest position in the spiritual plane.

21 Whatever a great man does, that other man also does (imitate); whatever he sets up as the standard, that the world (people) follow.

श्रेष्ठ व्यक्ति जो कुछ करता है, वही अन्य यानि साधारण जन भी करते है I वह जैसे प्रमाणित कर देता है, लोग उसी के अनुसार वर्तन करते है I”

Man is essentially an imitative animal. This is a psychological truth. The moral rejuvenation of society in any period of history can take place only because of the examples set by the leaders of that nation. Students can be disciplined only when the teachers are well-behaved. The minor officials cannot be kind and honest when the rulers of the country are corrupt and tyrannical. Children's behaviour depends entirely upon, and is ever controlled by, the standard of purity and culture of their parents.

With this, Krishna raises his next argument on why Arjuna should act in the world. Unless he diligently acts, the chances are that the entire community will follow the low standard of retreat from action set up by him, and thus they will ultimately invite a general decadence of culture in life. There is one danger with *Gyan*-Yogi because he is content and satisfied with the self *(Atama)*, tha common people try to follow the *Gyan*-Yogi and do not do any actions. Giving advice and following that advice is more effective for the common people. Therefore, *Gyan*-Yogi should not stop their *Karmas* even after attaining the knowledge of self, at least for society, according to B.G.Tilak, in Geeta Rahasya (गीता-रहस्य).

"If you doubt as it regards the necessity for working for the protection of the masses, why do you not observe me? Why do you not follow my example, and try to prevent the masses from going astray, setting up an example for them in yourself?"

22. There is nothing in the three worlds, O Partha, that has to be done by me, nor is there anything unattained that should be attained by me, yet, I enjoy myself in action.

हे पार्थ I तीनो लोको में मेरा कुछ भी कर्तव्य नही है, क्योकि न तो मुझे कुछ प्राप्त करना है I फिर भी मै कर्म में ही लगा रहता हु I

23. For, should I not ever engage Myself in action, without relaxation, men in every way follow my path, O son of Partha

क्योंकि, हे पार्थ, यदि मै कदाचित निद्रा-आलस छोड़कर कर्म में न लगा रहू, तब तो मनुष्य सब प्रकार से मेरे मार्ग का अनुसरण करेंगे I”

24. These worlds would perish if I don’t perform action; I would be the cause of confusion in the social structure and the destruction of mankind.

“यदि मै कर्म न करू, तो ये सारे लोक नष्ट-भ्रष्ट हो जायें, में वर्णसंकर का कर्ता होऊ तथा इन प्रजाओं कें ध्वस्त का कारन बनू I”

Performance of actions is not limited to mortals alone. Even God himself (Kings or highly reputed) is indirectly an active participant in this life cycle. Nothing is possible without His will. Birth and death, growth and decay, love and hate, pleasure and pain, wealth and poverty, rise and fall of civilisations, moment of planets, change of seasons: indeed, all activities that we see around us is a manifestation of His (means God or Almighty or Krishna) interest in the orderly functioning of the universe. If He were not involved, the world would come to an abrupt end, and HE would be the cause of its annihilation. None knows how he does this, but his unseen hand behind all that takes place is quite evident. Scientific reasoning can only explain how some of the natural phenomena take place, but many more are still beyond our comprehension. Our perception is limited to five sense-organs and the mind, but whatever falls beyond the scope of these six faculties becomes a mystery and falls in the realm of mysticism.

Why should the Lord (Krishna himself) work? What would be the loss to the generation if HE were not to work at all? The masses always imitate leaders and heroes in their dress, in their behaviour, in their moral values, in their actions, in all the branches of their activities. They fix their measure of perfection always by watching the standard of life of their leaders. If the Lord did not continue to work without relaxation, men also follow in His wake and sink themselves into inactivity and so into an unproductive existence. In nature, everything acts constantly and sincerely. The entire universe survives and sustains itself by activity.

Suppose, on the other hand, you, Arjuna, think – or for that matter, any other man thinks that one who has achieved his goal of self-realisation. Even then, he should work for the welfare of others, although for himself, he may have nothing to gain or achieve.

Learned and an ignoramus' way of working

25. As the 'ignorant' men act from attachment to action, O Bharata, so should the 'wise' men act without attachment, wishing for the welfare of the world.

> 'हे अर्जुन I कर्म में आसक्त हो अज्ञानी जन जिस तीव्रता से कर्म करते है, ज्ञानी को अनासक्त रहकर लोकसंग्रह अर्थात लोगों का हित करने की इच्छा से उसी तीव्रता के साथ (कर्म) करना चाहिए I"

Here Krishna says that a man of self-realisation also works in the world with as much diligence and sincerity, tireless enthusiasm and energising joy, burning hopes and scalding fears, as any ordinary man striving in the competitions of the marketplace. The intensity of the *Karmas* (actions) of the man-of-knowledge (आध्यात्मिक or spiritualist) is just like a common man or materialist. Both of them have a certain aim for the *Karmas*. The main difference is that the materialist does the actions with attachment (आसक्त) and desire-prompted actions.

Therefore, *Karmas* gets attached to him (materialistic), whereas the spiritualist does not have any desire or attachment for the actions. He (आध्यात्मिक) does *Karmas* for the society only; therefore, *Karma* does not get attached to the spiritualists.

A materialistic man does the actions by self-prompted motives, whereas the spiritualistic man does the actions for others. Self-prompted activities give the excitement (आसक्ति) and therefore, the action gets attached. But the actions done for others do not get attached, and there won't be any worries for actions. One should keep in mind that if any attachment is there for *Karmas*, then that also comes in selfishness. Therefore, *Karmas* should be done without any selfish motives for others, then such action does not get attached. There is one danger for spiritualists to leave the action, because after attaining the knowledge of self (*Atama*), he need not do any *Karmas*, but the *Tamssic* people take the example and they also abandon the *Karmas*, therefore Lord Krishna advises Arjuna that after attaining the Knowledge of self (*Atama*), *Gyan*-Yogi should do the actions with same intensity for the society.

In short, the spiritualist does the actions without attachment. After having the needful things in his life to support the materialistic body, he concentrates on the knowledge of *Atama* (self) and does the *Karmas* for others, whereas the materialist, even after fulfilling the materialistic needs, continues to do and tries to get more and more for himself.

26. Let no wise man unsettle the mind of ignorant people, who are attached to action; he should engage them all in actions himself, fulfilling them with devotion.

"ज्ञानी को चाहिए कि वह कर्म में आसक्त अज्ञानियो में बुद्धिभेद पैदा न करे अपितु स्वय योग में स्थित रह, समस्त कर्मो को अच्छी तरह करता हुआ उन सबको भी कर्म में लगाये रखे I"

In this stanza, the art of guiding mankind is given out, which can be used by every leader in all societies, be they social workers or political masters or cultural teachers. A society that is functioning in a particular line of activity at any given period of history should not be, all of a sudden, stopped in its flow or it's functioning, says Krishna. The leader should fall in line with the generation, and slowly and steadily guide it to act in the right direction, by his own example.

A traveller motoring with an idea of going to Haridwar may miss his way and speed down towards Lucknow, but the way to guide him back to the main road is not to halt him, because, by halting him, he will never reach his own destination, or any other goal. So long as the wheels are not revolving on the road, distances are not covered. Keeping the wheels on the move, he has to change the direction of his moments until he comes to his right path, heading towards Haridwar.

Similarly, man should act, and even if acting in the wrong direction, through action alone can he come to the RIGHT PATH of divine activities, and gain the fulfilment of his perfection. No wise man should unsettle his generation's firm faith in actions in a divine and better fashion, and he must make himself an example to the world, so that the lesser folk may automatically imitate him and learn to follow his unfailing footsteps.

Lord Krishna advises the wise (ज्ञानी) to get involved in *Karmas* himself and ask the ignorant (अज्ञानी) to do the *Karmas.* But the wise should have good conduct (सदाचरण). What does good conduct mean? Because the wise know where the action pinches or affects. The wise should give his knowledge to the ignorant and get involved continuously in *Karmas* as a *Karma*-Yogi (निष्काम) or without expecting the fruits of action. If a wise person is not involved in *Karma*-Yoga, then the ignorant cannot learn from the wise. Therefore, people who do Karmas for others or for society but might be ignorant in knowledge. Some people are wise and knowledgeable but not involved in *Karmas* like most of the Saints. However, there are very rare men, do *Karmas* for society, like Mahatma Gandhi or Ramakrishna. Lord Krishna is talking about such rare wise men in this Shaloka.

The wise (*Gyani*) have been advised to direct the ignorant to do all the *Karmas* (सर्वकर्म) and he also does the *Karmas*. What does it mean by all *Karmas*? All *Karmas* means without thinking whether the *Karmas* are right or wrong. It cannot be like this. In the Bhagwat-*Geeta, Karma* (action) has a definite meaning, and let us try to elaborate on the meaning of *Karmas*. *Karma* is of two types, one is good and another is bad. For bad *Karmas* it is defined as "विकरमा" which has been elaborated in chapter four (17) of the Bhagwat-*Geeta*. *Karma* which is not done due to Laziness or bad conduct is called "अकर्म." Good *Karmas* are also of two types: "सकाम" *Sakam-Karmas* and "निष्काम" *Nishkam-Karmas*. This means doing good actions and expecting fruits of action is called "सकाम" and good actions but without expecting fruits of action, called "निष्काम". For example, if I do the prayer to God for myself or for my family is called सकाम (*Sakam)* prayer, and if I do the prayer for society or for God itself, then it is called निष्काम (Nishkam) prayer. The wise (ज्ञानी) does the निष्काम *Nishkam* prayer. Here, all *Karma* means good *Karmas* only. Therefore, the wise should advise the ignorant to do all *Karmas*, and he himself should be involved in all *Karmas*. But for the ignorant it will be (सकाम) *Samam-Karmas*, and the same *Karmas* would be निष्काम *(Nishkam Karmas)* for the wise. The advantage of this is that the ignorant also learn to do the (निष्काम) *Nishkam Karmas* slowly (without expecting fruits of action) by seeing the wise man's *Karmas*.

As explained above, Lord Krishna directs the wise (ज्ञानी) to get himself involved in actions and set an example of *Karma*-Yoga in front of ignorant *Karmic* people. In context with Arjuna, He (Lord) says if you consider a wise (ज्ञानी), then do the war and set an example for the future generation. Here, the Lord is trying to establish a link between सकाम and निष्काम *Sakam and Nishkam Karmas*. Again, if you do only spiritual things, then wise become self-centred, which is also not good for society and if you are involved only in actions, that is also not good because you are concentrating on yourself and your family. Spirituality (निवृती) gives the direction for the *Karmas*, and aptitude (प्रव्रति) gives the speed for the *Karmas*. Therefore, a combination of both spiritual and material (निव्रती and प्रव्रति) is good for society and an ideal wise man (ज्ञान-योगी).

In what way is an ignorant man attached to action?

27. All actions are performed, in all cases, merely by the qualities-in-nature *(Gunas)*. He, whose mind is deluded by egoism, thinks "I am the doer".

> "प्रकृति के गुणों के द्वारा समस्त कर्म संपन होते है I अहंकार से विमूढ़ हुआ व्यक्ति ऐसा मानता है कि मै करता हु I"

We had explained earlier how the spiritual IGNORANCE expresses itself at the intellectual level as DESIRES, which again, in the mental zone, manifests as thoughts, and every thought, colored by our mental tendencies. How the mental tendencies are nucleated in the mind, which depends upon *Gunas (Karmas)* cultivated in the present and past life. If the *Gunas* are *Satvic* in nature, there are noble thoughts; there, noble actions manifest. When the mental tendencies are *Rajasic and Tamssic Gunas* in nature, the thoughts are agitated, and actions are also uncertain, fettering, and confused. And where the thoughts are dull and animalistic, the actions generated from them are correspondingly base, vicious and cruel. Thus, the mind's projections in the outer world are, in fact, a kind of crystallisation of the mental *Vasanas* among the objects of the world, and these constitute the 'actions'.

These actions are therefore, GENERATED by the mind, STRENGTHENED in the mind and ultimately PERFORMED with the mind. But the individual who has *Rajassic and Tamssic Gunas*, due to his wrong identification with his own mind, gets the false notion that he himself is the 'actor'. This action-arrogation EGO naturally starts feeling anxiety for its success and a burning attachment to the result of its actions. This identification with a mental condition creates the false sense of ego, which arrogates the demands of the fruits of his action. To get over this attachment is to end this misconception.

But what about for the wise man?

28. O mighty armed, the man of wisdom who can differentiate between the essence of qualities (*Gunas*) and their functions and who knows that the senses engage themselves in their objects is not attached to them.

> "परन्तु हे महाबाओ, गुण और कर्म के विषय में जाननेवाला तत्ववेता ऐसा मानता है कि परिनामरूप इन्द्रियाँ गुणों के ही परिनामरूप रूप-रसादि विषयों में बरत रही है और ऐसा समजकर वह आसक्त नही होता I"

The Lord says that *Karma*-yogi should do his actions without attachment to their rewards with the same zeal and devotion as an ignorant individual does with fruit in mind. The actions of *Karma*-Yogi are directed towards the welfare of society at large. Because of his noble deeds, he becomes an example to be emulated by others. Through his example, he keeps people away from wrongful activities. While explaining the basic concepts of *Karma*-yoga and the essence of true knowledge, he should not plant any seed of doubt or discontent in the minds of unsuspecting people. By his words and deeds, he should direct their energies to perform actions as a duty and not look for rewards.

Let us take an example of a *Sattvic* person. If he does some egoistic behaviour with his friend or colleagues, a man of wisdom of *Sattvic* nature, he thinks his behaviour was not good and tries to rectify it in future because he knows that during that situation his egoness dominated because of his *Gunas*. A man of knowledge tries to minimise his egotism and moves towards the perfection of life of spirituality. Whereas a deluded *Sattvic* person tries to give his justifications and does not learn.

Summarising in these two shlokas, the Lord tells the difference between the wise (ज्ञानी) and the idiot (मूढ़).

Actions are done by both, but the wise think the actions are done due to the characteristics of sense-organs, whereas the ignorant or idiot thinks he is the doer. Human nature (प्रकृति) is very much involved with sense-organs (इन्द्रिया), and each sense-organ has a particular function to do. These sense organs have all the time doing their functions. For example, when I open my eyes I always see, my ear always hears whatever falls on my ear and my skin always feels cold, hot, soft or hard whenever my skin comes in contact. Even if a man does not want to do any action, the sense organs do their functions. The man of knowledge (ज्ञानी) thinks it is the function of the sense-organs and does not get attached or involved in their functions. But he (*Gyani*) makes use of the sense-organs for the needful life's existence. For example, he does the sex and enjoys it but from inside (mind), he always thinks it is the nature of the sense organ and does not get attached (आसक्ति). The idiot (मूढ़) always thinks (अहंकार से) he is doing all these things, and his actions get attached with him.

29. Those deluded by the qualities of nature (*Gunas*), are attached to the functions of the qualities. The man of perfect knowledge should not unsettle the 'foolish' who are of imperfect knowledge.

> "प्रकृते के गुणों से मोहित हुए लोग गुणों के क्रियाओं में अर्थात देह और इन्द्रियों के व्यापारों में आसक्त होते है I ऐसे उन अल्पज्ञ मूढो को सम्पूर्ण तत्व का जाननेवाला ज्ञानी विचलित न करे I"

Although many know that all actions are attempts of the mental impressions *(Gunas)* to fulfil themselves in the outer world, only the perfect one realises this truth and generally becomes quiet and unattached in all his activities. The majority of us are in a state of complete delusion and are entirely victimised by our mental temperaments (*Gunas)*. The advice given by Krishna in the earlier stanza (25) is, again for emphasis, repeated here in different words.

The dull-witted ones (*Tamssic and Rajssic*), unconsciously victimised by their own mental impressions, act in the world outside, shackled by thousands of burning attachments. A man of perfect knowledge (Sage or Saint) should not come into the arena of life to decry (criticise) such a man's activities all of a sudden. Krishna's suggestion is that, while feeding (advising) the fire of life, he (wise man) should carefully guide (*Tamssic or Rajssic*) their flow into the right channel (direction) wherein the flood of life can reach to water the garden of cultural development in the individual as well as in the community.

In these two shlokas, the Lord tells the difference between the wise (ज्ञानी) and the idiot (मूढ़). Actions are done by both, the wise think the actions are done due to the characteristics of the sense-organs whereas the ignorant or idiot thinks he is the doer. In this shloka, the Lord refers to the foolish as imperfectly knowledgeable (मन्द) and the wise as perfectly knowledgeable. The imperfect knowledge is not farsighted but think in the short term. In this shloka, such dull-witted people are full of ego and attachment and involved in the sense-organ-satisfied Karmas. Therefore, the completely knowledgeable (*Gyanis)* should not disturb them by telling the spiritual knowledge. In stanza 26 also referred to almost the same thing for the wise, but there it was advised on the basis of materialistic *Karmas* for less-intelligent or dull people. If a perfectly knowledgeable (*Gyani*) gives advice to the dull (मन्द), then two things happen. Firstly, they (मन्द-बुद्धि) do not understand the knowledge and interpret it in the wrong ways. Secondly, if they understand, then they do not do any *Karmas* (अकर्म) and become lazy. The net result would be for dull people, they are neither this side nor that side (ना इधर के ना उधर के) or (निशंकू). In such conditions, how these dull-witted people (मन्द) can be improved is given in the following shloka.

30. Renouncing all actions in me, with the mind centred on the self (*Atama*), free from hope and egoism, free from (mental) fever, (you) do fight.

“सभी कर्मों को मुझमें समर्पित करते हुए, चित्त को आत्मा में केन्द्रित कर आशारहित, ममतारहित और सन्तापरहित से युद्ध कर I”

In earlier Shlokas, Lord Krishna has explained the difference between the wise and unwise, ethical and unethical, egoistic and egoless persons. In this Shloka,

He explains that the wise person should do the actions himself, and he (wise) should promote the unwise to do the actions. The difference between the two is that the wise, due to his spiritual nature he does not think he is a doer, whereas the unwise thinks he is a doer because of his ego. Therefore, the *Karmas* get attached to the unwise. In this Shloka, He (Krishna) tells Arjuna to do the *Karmas* for the society. Although in Shloka 20, He has given hints for society work. But in this stanza, He explains in detail how to conduct the social work.

Anybody can do social work, but one has to conduct their *Karmas* according to their nature (instinct). For example, the king Arjuna has been trained in fighting and also his background so his instinct (स्वधर्म) is to fight. A teacher's instinct (स्वधर्म) is teaching, and a labourer's instinct is to do hard work, whereas a businessman's instinct is business. Anybody can do social work (लोकसंग्रह) for the society, provided they keep the following points in their mind.

If anybody's *Karmas* go through the following five filtrations, then that work (action) becomes social.

1. Dedicate the actions to the Almighty.
2. Before undertaking any actions or work, think through your inner consciousness (self). That means your mind should be pure and concentrate on yourself.

3. Hope (आशारहित) or don't concentrate on the fruits of action. But just keep an aim for the future but concentrate on the *Karmas* in the present.

4. Attachment (ममतारहित) should be minimal with materialistic bodies and with actions.

5. The anger should be minimal. Ego is responsible for the anger. If ego is minimum, the anger also will be minimum, where one can take the right decision for the *Karmas.*

If your actions go through these five steps, then it becomes social work (लोकसंग्रह). Another advantage of such actions is that it does not have any binding on the doer, and they promote others also to do such actions. Such *Karmas* become an example for others and help for the refinement of society.

Hope is the child of the unborn future; ego is the lingering memory of the dead past. To live (revel) in the ego and hope is an attempt on our part to live, either with the dead moments of the past, or with the unborn moments of the future. All the while, the tragedy is that we miss the 'present', the active dynamics 'present', which is only the noble chance that is given to us to create, to advance, to achieve and to enjoy. Krishna advises that Arjuna should renounce all actions unto the Lord and, getting rid of both hope and selfishness, must fight free from mental fever.

The term 'fight' is to be understood here as our fight with circumstances, in the silent battle of life. Thus, the advice is not for Arjuna alone, but to all men who would like to live life fully and intelligently.

31. Those men who constantly practice this teaching of mine, full of faith and without cavilling (objection), are also freed from actions.

"जो मनुष्य श्रद्धापूर्वक, दोषद्रष्टि न रखते हुए, मेरे इस मत के अनुसार नित्य बर्तते है, वे भी कर्मो से छुट जाते है I"

In the above Shloka, it was shown that what type of *Karmas* become social and such *Karmas* become *Akarmic* (अकर्मिक). But the devotees who have not reached this state and who do their actions with inner-consciousness (self) without any attachment and dedicate their *Karmas* to the Almighty with full faith, they also get rid of *Karma*.

Krishna tells Arjuna that whoever above teachings follows and practices in their life regularly, having full faith in him (Lord) without any objections, will also be freed from sin and sinless *Karmas*. Absence of all desires can come only when we rediscover the All-full nature of the self (*Atama*). In short, with the knowledge of the self, when the spiritual 'Ignorance' is terminated, desires can no longer arise. Thus, the term 'FREED

FROM WORK' indicates the state beyond 'ignorance,' or the state of selfhood (knowing *Atama*).

This supreme state, no doubt, can never be reached purely through work. Parliament Street is not the parliament, but having reached Parliament Street, the parliament cannot be very far away; one cannot miss reaching parliament there. Similarly, *Karma*-Yoga is extolled here as the 'path' that takes one ultimately to the supreme, because through desireless activity one achieves *Vasana*-Purgation, thus making the mind purer and subtler for meditative purposes.

What happens to those who do not follow his teachings?

32. But those who carp at my teaching and do not practice it, deluded in all knowledge, and devoid of discrimination, know them to be doomed to destruction.

"परन्तु जो मेरे इस मत में दोष निकालते हुए उसके अनुसार नही बर्तते, उन लोगों को तू सब प्रकार के ज्ञान मोहित, अविवेकी और कल्याण के पथ से भ्रष्ट हुआ ही जान I"

"Those who decry (denounce) this great teaching of mine and do not practice it", Krishna warns his students, 'Will become more and more deluded and will lose their discrimination.' The discrimination faculty is divine in human beings because of which man is considered superior to animals. An intelligence, strengthened by its own intrinsic capacity to distinguish between the Real and the Unreal, the Right and the Wrong, is the mighty instrument of self-development in man. When this instrument is destroyed, man comes to behave in no better way than a bipedal animal; painting on the path of existence, bullied by its own lower instincts of miserable passions and low appetites. Naturally, he fails to make any true gain out of his life's chances, and finally destroys himself.

Work against one's nature

What could be the reasons for not following your teachings and practising them?

33. Even a wise man acts in accordance with his own nature; beings will follow their own nature; what can restraint do?

"कईबार ज्ञानी भी अपने निज के स्वभाव के अनुरूप चेष्टा करता है I सभी प्राणी स्वभाव का ही अनुवर्तन करते है I इसमें निग्रह (restraint) भला क्या करेगा?"

The man of knowledge indicates one who has read and understood thoroughly the technique of action as explained in this chapter. Even when he knows the technique, the Lord says that it is not easy for him to follow it, because his mind (i.e. spirit with past *Karmas*) is so strong and designed to carry his thoughts. Because of these past impressions (वासना *or Gunas*), even an honest student finds it hard to practice this simple-looking technique in his life. The reason is quite universal. "Beings follow their own nature (*Gunas*)." Naturally, "what can restraint do" when nature (particular *Gunas*) is too powerful even in the man of knowledge. Who can then restrain the unwise person?

This last statement in the stanza, "what can restraint do" is not a cry of despair in Krishna's philosophy. It is the honest, all-seeing vision of the philosopher in Krishna, who recognises that the higher ways of living are not meant for all, even very few men of wisdom can follow. Men crowding (many) on the lowest rung of the evolutionary ladder, overwhelmed by their own animal passions, find themselves incapable of renouncing them, and are, therefore, incapacitated to walk the path of action. It is only a slightly evolved entity, full of enthusiasm, activity and a passion for progress (*Sattva-Guna*), who can follow this sacred 'path' and benefit itself. This honest confession shows the broad-mindedness and tolerance of Krishna, the universal teacher.

If every being acts according to his own nature (past *Gunas*), then there is no scope for further improvement, and teaching becomes purposeless. The Lord explains as follows:

34. Attachment (liking) and aversion of the objects of the senses abide in the senses; let none come under their sway, for they are his foes.

"इन्द्रयों का अपने विषयों के प्रति राग और द्वेष स्वाभाविक है, किसी को इस राग और द्वेष में नही आना चाहिए, क्योकि ये दोनों उसके (कल्याण-मार्ग में विग्न डालनेवाले) शत्रु है I"

Krishna indicates here the great robber in the 'within' of man, which loots away the true joys and thrills of 'right living'. Attachments (liking) and aversions (strong dislike) of the sense-organs for their respective sense-objects are instinctive and natural in everyone. The sense-objects, by themselves, are incapable of bringing any wave of sorrow or agitation into 'within'. We get agitated and disturbed not at our sense-organs, but in our mind, which accepts, in its inherent mischief, certain types of stimuli as GOOD and their opposite as BAD. Good stimuli to the sense-organ create happiness, and bad stimuli create unhappiness. But happiness and unhappiness are independent of each other. Eyes' function is to see the things which can be seen, good and bad. The ears' function is to hear the sound. A pleasant and good sound creates happiness, and a bad sound creates unhappiness. Similarly, all sense-organs create happiness and anger. Lord Krishna advises here that we should not think that it is the function of sense-organs, but we should try to restrain or channalise the sense-organs, right from the beginning, otherwise the sense-organs become uncontrollable and a source of unhappiness. The only insistence is that on all occasions, a wise man should be a master of the vehicles and not a helpless victim of these matter-envelopments. And the secret of this mastery in life is to live free from the tyrannies of likings and aversions of the sense organs.

35. Better is one's 'duty' though devoid of merit, than the 'duty' of another well discharged. Better is the death in one's own 'duty'; the 'duty' of another is fraught with fear (is productive of positive danger).

> "दूसरों का कर्म (कर्तव्य) अच्छा लगने के बाजूद, अपने स्वधर्म कर्म में ही रहना श्रेयस्कर होता है I दुसरे के कर्म करने से बहुदा असफलता ही होती है I स्वधर्म में रहना (मरना) हमेशा परधर्म से बेहतर होता है I"

That which determines one man's personality as distinctly different from another's is, texture of the thoughts entertained by him. This texture of his thoughts is again, in its own turn, determined by the pattern of thinking (वासना), which his mind has gained from his own past *Gunas.* These predetermined 'channels-of-thinking' created by one's own earlier ways of thinking are called वासना (*Gunas*). In its right import, *Swadharma* (स्वधर्म) means the type of वासना (इम्प्रेशंस) *(Gunas*) that one discovers in one's mind. To act according to one's taste, inborn and natural, is the only known method of living in peace and joy, in success and satisfaction. To act against the grain of one's own *Vasanas* would be acting in terms of *Par-Dharma* that this is fraught with danger is very well known. There could be one more reason to do another's duty due to fear and greed, but it generally ends with failure.

In the context of *Geeta*, there is a direct message for Arjuna. Arjuna is born a prince, trained in the art of war and has exhibited in life his insatiable thirst for heroism and adventure. Naturally, his *Swadharma* (वासना) is that of a prince and that can find fulfilment only in dangerous actions and endless exertions. Perhaps, as it is evident in the first chapter, Prince Arjuna had gathered during his early education, that the life of renunciation and meditation – the life of *Brahman* – was nobler than his own life. Therefore, he wanted to run away from the battlefield into the silent caves of meditation. The life of *Brahman* (knowledge) would have been easier for Udhishter, his elder brother, as he had in the past life (प्रबध-कर्मा) *Brhman Karmas* but not for him and Bhima. Krishna reminds him that to act according to his own *vasanas*, even imperfectly, is the right path of his development. It is dangerous to suppress his own personality-expression and copy the activities of someone else, even if he is living a nobler and diviner life.

Arjuna said:

36. O, Varshney, then why does a man commit sin, though reluctantly, as if compelled by some force?

“अर्जुन बोला – हे कृष्ण I अब किसके द्वारा परिचालित होकर यह मनुष्य न चाहते हुए भी बलपूर्वक लगाया गया-सा पाप करता है I”

The disciple (Arjuna) now asks a definite question upon the very theme of discussion. The very question shows that Arjuna has, to a large extent, got out of the hasty conclusion which is exhibited until the beginning of the second chapter. He has become introspective, and therefore, conscious of certain workings within himself that were running and obstructing the play of his own higher impulses. The doubt is couched in such familiar words that it appears as though it was a doubt raised by some student of our own times.

In spite of all that has been said above, it is not uncommon to find people attracted to evil. They move in this direction as if driven by an invisible force beyond their control.

In this stanza, Arjuna asks the question as to why this happens. The Lord says: Listen. I shall tell you who that enemy is of whom you ask – who is the source of all evil:

Desire and Anger are the Real Enemies

The Blessed Lord said:

37. Know that the enemy in this regard is the desire **(काम or intense desire)**, it is the same as the anger which is born of *Rajssic* qualities. This enemy is never satisfied with the objects of the senses and is extremely wicked.

"श्री भगवान बोले – यह काम है, यह क्रोध है, जो रजोगुण से उत्पन हुआ है I यह महापेटू और बड़ा पापी है I इस संसार में इसे अपना शत्रु जान I"

The intense desire (कामना) is the main culprit. If the intense desire is satisfied, then it does not stop. It (desire) wants more and more, which is never satisfied.

If the intense desire is abstracted, the intense anger (क्रोध) is created, and in this intense anger, his discriminating power is lost, and he can do anything, including the killing of his own parents, wife or any near and dear things, or kill himself.

Whenever emotions for the acquisition and possession of an object flow incessantly *(Rajssic)* towards that object, the bundle of thoughts so flowing in is called 'intense-Desire'; while the same emotions, when they get obstructed from reaching their desired objects, and get refracted at the intermediate obstacle, are called 'Anger'. This 'desire-anger-emotion' is the very SATAN in us that compels us to compromise with our own intellectually known higher values of existence, and tempts us to perpetrate sins. The greater the desire, the greater will be the power in the pull towards the sinful and the low. Once desire has come to manifest itself in our intellect, it enshrouds the wisdom in us.

Desire (काम) and anger (क्रोध), and their numberless children of sin and sorrow, must ever come to breed upon the marshy lands of our deluded intellect. To come under their sway (influence) is 'ignorance'. To come to rule over them is 'wisdom'. Desire is not created by God or fate or circumstances or time, but man himself alone.

Now the question arises, humans have the inner consciousness which is a part of Almighty. Does it mean that this intense desire (कामना) is so powerful it veils the inner consciousness also? The Lord now illustrates how intense desire is our FOE (enemy) and how it veils our discrimination:

38. As fire is enveloped by smoke, as a mirror by dust, as an embryo by the womb, so this wisdom is enveloped by that desire or anger (काम या क्रोध).

> "जिस प्रकार आग धुएँ से ढकी रहती है, जिस प्रकार दर्पण धुल-मैल के द्वारा ढका रहता है तथा जिस प्रकार गर्भ जेर से ढका रहता है, उसी प्रकार उस कामना (desire) के द्वारा यह विवेकरूप ज्ञान ढका रहता है I"

39. Enveloped, O son of Kunti, is 'wisdom' by this constant enemy of the wise in the form of 'desire' which is difficult to appease (pacify).

> "हे कुन्तीपुत्र अर्जुन I ज्ञानी की चिरशत्रु इस कामरूप और कभी न तृप्त होनेवाली अग्नि के द्वारा ढका रहता है I"

We know that our attachments to things can fall under three distinct categories. Our desires can either be low and high (Vicious) – mind for craving – (1) fleshly carnal pleasures, (2) our ambitions may be for an active exertion to achieve power and wealth, to gain strength, and (3) might, to strive and achieve a diviner perfection and Godly self-illumination. Thus, our desires can fall under three headings according to the quality of the attachment: inert (*Tamssic*), active (*Rajssic*), or noble and divine (*Sattvic*). The veils that are created over our discrimination by these different types of qualities (*Gunas*) are indicated here by the three different examples.

Lord Krishna tells Arjuna that human beings have consciousness, but the intense desire (कामना) covers the consciousness like smoke to the fire, dust to the mirror and womb to the embryo and hence his knowledge is veiled. The desire has mainly three forms. The first one is that one can get the desire (सूक्ष्म) by seeing or hearing from somebody. If that thing appeals, then one wants to acquire it. In this stage, such desire can be removed easily, just like blowing air to the smoke (chimney) so that the fire gives more heat. If you want to have that desire, the second stage is called crystallisation (स्थूल) of desire, which means whether it is possible for you to acquire or out of reach. Even in the second stage, one can get rid of desire just like removing dust from the mirror. But if you want to satisfy that desire, then comes the third stage called intense desire (अतिस्थुल), where it is very difficult to get rid of such desire just like an embryo in the womb. The embryo is not visible until it matures in the womb. The intense desire (कामना) completely covers your consciousness and tries to satisfy that desire again and again, and cannot think what is right and what is wrong.

Therefore, in Shloka 39, Lord Krishna tells Arjuna that this intense desire (काम) ruins even a man of wisdom (ज्ञानी-पुरुष) and He says it (desire) is never satisfied. If we think little about such desire, we are entangled in more and more thinking, and we get very easily from the first stage to the third stage and ruin ourselves.

He now tells us which are the seats of 'Desires' which, by enveloping wisdom, form the enemy of the world. If the seat of the enemy is known, it is easy to kill it.

40. The senses, the mind and the intellect are said to be its seat; through these, it deludes the embodied, by veiling his wisdom.

"इन्द्रियाँ, मण और बुद्धि इस काम (intense-desire) के रहने के स्थान कहे जाते है I इनके द्वारा यह कामना देही के ज्ञान को ढक लेता है और उसे मोहित करता है I”

A true criminal, functioning as an efficient leader of a gang, operating in a large area, will generally have more than one place to function from. Three main offices, from where 'desire', in different forms, functions to destroy the peace and health in our inner life, have been indicated here very clearly. **Firstly**, the sense-organs, functioning without restraint in the world of sense-objects, are a very convenient theatre for 'desire' to function in. **Secondly**, the external stimuli, when they reach the mind through sense-organs, the mind also becomes the breeding centre of sorrows created by 'desire.' **Thirdly**, the intellect, working and playing with memories of the sense-enjoyments it had lived, and of the mental attachments it had entertained, becomes yet another safe haven for 'desire' to function from.

The deluded ego, foolishly identifying with the body, desires sense-enjoyments. Thoughtlessly identifying with the mind, it thirsts to experience more and more emotional satisfactions. Lastly, identifying with intellect, it plans to re-live the remembered experiences of sense-enjoyments and mental-joys.

If we know the places of the enemy where they stay, then it becomes easy to kill them. The places of intense desire (कामना) are the sense-organs, mind and the intellect. This intense desire covers the knowledge of discrimination and tries to satisfy the ego of a man. As described in the above Shloka, the intense desire (काम) is created in three stages. The first stage of desire (सूक्ष्म-अवस्था) originates through the sense-organs. If he likes the object through the sense organs, then the signal goes to the mind. In the first stage itself, the desire can be arrested or stopped by force (दम-से). If he wants to have the object, the signal goes to the mind that is called more desire (स्थुल-अवस्था). If the mind also likes that object, then it plans how to execute it. The mind sends the signal to action-organs for execution, without sending the signal to the intellect, which we call emotional thinking. Here at this stage, generally, we make the wrong decision. If the mind does not like it, then it can be stopped by will-power (शम-से). The function of the mind is just like a CPU, and it does not make any decision, but it receives the signals from sense-organs and sends them back, if we don't like it. If we like it, then it sends to the action-organs or to the intellect. If the signal is sent to the intellect, then it (intellect) decides whether the object is likeable or not, with the memories or from somebody else (friends or well-wishers). If the intellect gives its approval, called intense desire (अतिस्थुल-अवस्था or काम), then the signal goes to the mind again, and the mind sends that signal to action organs for execution. If the intellect does not give its approval by using its *Atama* (आत्मा) or consciousness (विवेक-बुद्धि), the desired object can be stopped or arrested by using will-power (शम-से) and consciousness (दम, शम, and विवेक-बुद्धि से). As such, the intense desire's residence is in the mind after getting the approval from the intellect, but it (desire) is in the dormant condition (asleep) in the mind. If the desired object comes in front of the sense-organ, then the desire awakens and starts working through the action organs. If you want to get rid or remove this intense desire (काम), you have to remove forcefully or by strong will-power from the mind. To remove this desire from your mind, you have to divert your mind to some other aim. For example, if you are a scientist, divert your mind to scientific invention, and if you are a doctor, divert your mind or thinking to your profession. If you are a farmer or labourer, divert your attention to the chosen almighty (God). The diversion of the mind cannot happen in one day, but one has to do continuously and slowly, your mind can be diverted from intense desire (कामना).

If the intense desire makes the residence in your intellect (बुद्धि), then it becomes very difficult to remove it because you have accepted this desire as your friend. The desire can be removed if you consider it as your enemy; then only this desire (कामना) can be removed. The intense desire can be removed until it is in the mind because the intellect (बुद्धि) always gives you a warning. Once this desire goes into your intellect, then it becomes impossible to remove and you think it is a part of life.

How to finally overcome this inner enemy 'desire' is described in the following Shloka.

41. Therefore, O best of the Bharata, controlling first the senses, kill this sinful thing, the destroyer of knowledge and wisdom.

"हे भरतवंशी I इसलिए तू पहले इन्द्रिया को संयम कर,
ज्ञान और विज्ञान का नाश करनेवाले इस पापी काम (intense-desire)
को मार ही डाल I"

Krishna tells Arjuna, first restrain the senses, so that you may finally throw overboard the inner enemy 'intense desire' (काम). Desire is called sinful, since, in its grosser manifestations, it tends to make us live and work satisfying our lower nature, and thus persuades us to live a lower devolutionary life. Even at its best (*Sattvic*), like the smoke that covers the fire, 'desire' does not allow the full dawn of the infinite, which is the *Atama* (self) in us. Thus, 'desire' in all its textures, contributes to the sins of man; therefore, it is styled here as the SINFUL THING. Even desire for sense-objects can veil (covers) your knowledge and science of knowledge, therefore first control your senses.

Overcoming the Desire

Where should one take one's stand, and cast off the desires?

42. They say that the senses are superior to the body; superior to the senses is the mind; superior to the mind is the intellect; one who is superior to the intellect is HE (the *Atama* or the self).

"इन्द्रियों को शरीर से शेष्ठ कहते है, मन इन्द्रियों से श्रेष्ठ है और बुद्धि मन
से श्रेष्ठ है, परन्तु जो बुद्धि से भी परे है, वह आत्मा है I"

43. Realising that He (the *Atama*) is superior (subtler) to intellect; controlling the mind through reason, destroy this enemy in the form of intense desire (काम) which is otherwise difficult to conquer.

> "हे महाबाहु अर्जुन I इस प्रकार आत्मा को बुद्धि से परे जानकर अपने आप को अपने द्वारा नियंत्रित करके इस दुर्जन कामरूप (intense-desire) शत्रु को मार डाल I"

In these two Shlokas, the importance of body, sense-organs, mind, intelligence and self is depicted. Although all the parts of the living body are important, here from the spiritual point of view, the importance is shown. Many wise people have interpreted these two shlokas in different ways, but we shall try to see here the importance from the spiritual point of view in the present situation. Here, the importance of all body parts is shown from the thinking point of view (साधना). The sense organs are superior to the materialistic body, because the body lights up due to sense organs. For instance, if your ears are blocked or not working, then the sound has no importance to the body, similarly, the other sense organs. Therefore, the sense organs are superior to the body. Then comes the mind, which is superior to the sense organs because if the mind does not respond to the senses, then the signal does not go to the mind. For example, if you are hearing your favourite music, even if a good or bad scene comes in front of you then your mind does not respond to the eyes because your mind is occupied by the music. Therefore, your mind is superior to the sense organs. However, the mind does the analysis part of the sense-organ signal, but it does not have the capacity to make a decision whether a particular signal is bad or good. The mind is just like a CPU in the computer world. The decision is taken by the intelligence (बुद्धि), and this decision signal is sent back to the mind for further processing. This means intelligence is superior to the mind (मनह). However, the intelligence is not the top-most part but the self (*Atama*), because the intelligence does not have its own consciousness (चेतना). Consciousness comes from the self to the intelligence. It (intelligence or बुद्धि) can refer to the self or not and can directly send the decision signal to the mind for execution. However, if the intelligence consults the self (आत्मा) through the mind, then it would be good or spiritual thinking. And if it does not consult the self, then it would be egoistic or desire (कामना) prompted thinking.

Now it is established that the self (*Atama*) is the highest thinking process because the intellect does not have its own consciousness. The intense desire (कामना) can come only up to the intellect. Therefore, Krishna advises in Shloka 43 that you eliminate this intense desire by *Atamic* (self)-thinking (अधात्मिक-विचार से). What does it mean by self-thinking? First, you think from inner consciousness and reach the mind, then you feel your body, sense organs, mind, and intellect light up with consciousness. Establishing self-thinking, the wavering of your mind and intellect stops, and the inner-consciousness from self (*Atama*) will be reflected, and you will be able to kill this intense desire (कामना) from your thinking.

Here Lord Krishna says that the desire (काम) is an enemy which is very difficult to control, and why is it difficult? Because this desire can come in different forms, if it (कामना) comes, as an enemy (बुराई) then it is not difficult to control. But, if it comes as a friend (भलाई), then the first thing is to recognise it because even the consciousness task becomes tough and it takes a longer time to recognise this desire. Nowadays, such examples are seen in politicians quite commonly. The Lord tells Arjuna that you are a good fighter (महाबाहु), having courage and consciousness.

In conclusion (उपसंहार), the Lord Krishna emphasises in the third chapter that a human being cannot leave without *Karmas* (action) even for a moment. Therefore, one should do the *Karmas* and his *Karmas* should be sacrificial form (यज्ञ), which becomes *Karma*-Yoga. The whole materialistic world is continuously engaged in sacrificial *Karmas*, and we also should become a part of this world by doing sacrificial *Karmas*. While doing such *Karmas*, doer (कर्तापन) and the beneficiary (भोक्तापन) do not remain, and such *Karmas* become *Akarmic* (अकरमिक), and by living in this materialistic world ([illegible]), we can spend a peaceful life. In our peaceful life, the intense desire (कामना) becomes the hindrance which can be eliminated by inner-consciousness (आध्यात्मिक), and we can decide whether our ruler can be intense desire (Ego or काम) or the self (*Atama*).